My Ideal
Jesus, Son of Mary

My Ideal
Jesus, Son of Mary

By

Father Emil Neubert, S.T.D.
Marianist

According to the spirit of
Father William Joseph Chaminade
Founder of the Marianists

A Translation Completely Revised
under the Author's Supervision

THIRD ENGLISH EDITION

TAN BOOKS AND PUBLISHERS, INC.
Rockford, Illinois 61105

| Imprimi Potest: | Peter A. Resch, S.M. |
| | Provincial Superior |

| Nihil Obstat: | William M. Drumm |
| | Censor Librorum |

Imprimatur:	Joseph E. Ritter
	Archbishop of St. Louis
	December 21, 1946

Library of Congress Catalog Card No.: 88-50578

ISBN: 0-89555-338-4

Third English Edition

| 9th Printing, May 1963 | 205th Thousand |
| 10th Printing, Sept. 1988 | 235th Thousand |

Printed and bound in the United States of America.

TAN BOOKS AND PUBLISHERS, INC.
P.O. Box 424
Rockford, Illinois 61105

1988

Maria Duce!

"Under Mary's Leadership!"

PUBLISHING HISTORY

My Ideal: Jesus, Son of Mary has been published in the following languages as of 1963: French (8th edition), Italian (5th), Dutch (4th), German (4th), English (3rd), Spanish (2nd), Polish (1st), Japanese (1st), Hungarian (1st), Slovak (1st), Catalonian (1st), Vietnamese (1st), Malayalam (1st), Chinese (1st), Portuguese (1st). Translations in preparation as of 1963: Croatian, Slovene, Lettonian, Hindi, Arabic, Zulu, Gaelic, Basque, Minor Breton, Ukrainian, and Congolese.

CONTENTS

PART 3—MARY EXPLAINS
TRANSFORMATION INTO JESUS

PART 4—MARY DESCRIBES HER SOLDIER

APPENDIX

PREFACE

The Christian who aims at perfection endeavors to imitate Jesus Christ as completely as possible. Among all the traits of the Divine Model one of the most beautiful to imitate is His filial piety to Mary our Mother—His Mother and ours.

My Ideal has been found to be an efficient aid in this Marian program of life. It leads to a firm, virile, intimate devotion of consecration to the Blessed Mother. It is presently treasured by many priests, sisters, brothers and lay people, young and old, as a blueprint for a Christian way of life under the aegis of Mary Immaculate.

The present edition is an attempt at a wider propagation of this spiritual teaching of Father Chaminade on Mary's part in our soul-life. It is a practical manual for sodalities, Catholic Action groups, schools, novitiates, and seminaries. The chapters are suited for reading, study, and meditation on the days of May and October.

My Ideal
Jesus, Son of Mary

*"I have given you an example, that
as I have done, so you do also."*
— (cf. John 13:15)

I

"I have given you the example..."

JESUS:

My brother, you love My Blessed Mother and you are glad to love her. But your love for her is far from what I would like it to be.

You love her because it is natural to love what is pure and beautiful, and she is ideally pure and beautiful.

1. You love her because it is natural to love those who are good and helpful, and no one is better or more helpful than she.

You love her because you regard her as a Mother and because every child loves its mother.

You love her because you have felt the influence of her love and have found out that with her you succeed more easily in keeping your purity and fervor.

You love her because you have learned from books and sermons that devotion to her is the easiest way of assuring your salvation and the surest way of attaining perfection—and you wish above all to save and sanctify yourself.

2. All these motives of love are good, but there is another much more excellent. These can serve as a foundation for a tender devotion to My Mother; they do not, however, lay the foundation for that devotion which I wish you to practice. Devotion to My Mother is something so important, so beneficial to you, so acceptable to her and to Me, that you cannot be satisfied with something mediocre, or good enough, or even very good, but solely with what is perfect.

3. Do you know the most perfect kind of devotion to Mary?

Search in books, consult theologians, ask the greatest servants of Mary that the earth has ever produced for the secret—and you will find nowhere a devotion more perfect than the one which I am going to teach you and which consists in *sharing in My own filial love for My Mother.*

Does not perfection for My disciples consist in being like their Master? Have I not given them the example, that, as I have done, they should also do? Did not My Apostle Paul repeat again and again that everything, for them, consists in imitating Christ, in clothing themselves with Christ, in taking on the dispositions of Christ, in living no longer their own life but the life of Christ?

Tell Me, can you imagine any more perfect dispositions toward My Mother than Mine?

THE FAITHFUL SOUL:

O Jesus, what a supremely charming prospect: to share in Your filial love for Your Mother! But, poor sinner that I am, how can I attain such an ideal? How can I even understand it?

2

I Am Mary's Son Because I Willed It!

JESUS:

My brother, to understand My filial love for My Mother, you must understand, first of all, that I am the Son of Mary because I deliberately chose that condition.

1. I did nothing by constraint, or by chance, or without a purpose.

When I decided to restore the glory of My Father and to save humanity, an infinite number of ways lay open before Me. To all others, however, I preferred the way of Mary.

I freely and deliberately created Mary to be My Mother, for she would not have been brought into existence had I not willed to confide this office to her: freely and deliberately I made her what she is, so that she might in turn make Me what I am.

In all truth I am her Child and I willed to be formed of My Mother's substance like every other child. I wanted to be nursed by her; I wanted to be brought up and cared for by her; I wanted to be entirely subject to her.

I am her Child much more truly than you are your mother's child, for from her alone I willed to derive My whole humanity.

I am her Child entirely, God and Man, because the One to whom she gave birth forms a single, undivided Person.

2. Now, I want you to realize that in choosing

to be her Child I was motivated by love: first of all, by love for My Heavenly Father, whom I could glorify more and whom men would understand and love more because of her; then, too, by love for My Mother, who was to give Me more joy than all angels and men together; and also, by love for men—in particular for you, My beloved brother.

III

Contemplate and Admire

JESUS:

Contemplate now what My filial love has inspired Me to do for My Mother.

1. From all eternity I thought of her and loved her, for from all eternity I saw in her My future Mother.

I thought of her when creating the heavens and the angels; I thought of her as I formed the earth and the human race.

I thought of her as I pronounced sentence against your first parents; I thought of her as I revealed Myself to the ancient patriarchs and prophets.

2. Out of love I heaped privileges upon her, each of which exceeds the greatest of My bounties toward all other creatures. I exempted her from laws to which the whole human race is subject: her alone did I make Immaculate in her Conception, free from all concupiscence, unsullied by any imperfection, more full of grace than all the angels and Saints,

Mother of God and ever a Virgin, glorified in her body, even as I was, before the general Resurrection.

3. Although I came on earth to redeem the human race, I gave thirty years of My life to Mary alone and three years to the rest of humanity.

4. Nor was I content to have her share My privileges and live in intimacy with Me; I willed that she should also have a part in the very mission which My Father had entrusted to Me. I, the Redeemer, determined that she should be the Co-Redemptrix with Me, and that everything which I merited for the Salvation of the world because it was strictly due to Me, she should merit too because it was supremely fitting.

5. I also willed that she should be associated with me even in Heaven. I willed that, as I am an advocate with the Father, she should likewise be an advocate with Me, in order to distribute all graces to men, because she cooperated with Me in gaining them. For, in Heaven even as on earth, I am her Son, and I am infinitely happy to reward her liberally for all that she formerly suffered and did in love for Me.

6. Listen further: I live in the Church; that is, in My Mystical Body directed by My Spirit. What the Church does is really done by Me; what the Church does for My Mother, is really being done for her by Me. Think of all the veneration and love the Church has shown her: the defense and proclamation of her privileges, the institution of feasts and devotions in her honor, the approval of confraternities and religious societies destined

to serve her. Think over the piety of the Church's children: of the Saints, who were all so devoted to My Mother; of fervent souls, who are drawn more and more to honor her in a special way; of the ordinary faithful themselves, who are so watchful over her honor, so clear-minded in recognizing her privileges (sometimes even more so than learned men), so enthusiastic the moment there is question of giving her some special mark of affection. What is all that if not a grand and yet quite imperfect manifestation of My own incomparable filial love toward My Mother?

To all that the Church Militant has done and will do for Mary down to the end of time, add what the Church Triumphant does for her throughout eternity; for I live even more in the Saints of Heaven than I do in the faithful on earth. Imagine the gratitude, respect and love which the blessed unceasingly manifest to their Queen and Mother, to whom they owe their eternal felicity. In them and by them, remember, it is always I who honor and love My Mother.

7. Pass in review these proofs of My filial love; delve into them, sound their depths, try to understand all you can about them, and notice that what you cannot understand surpasses infinitely anything you ever will understand of them. Then, say to yourself that it is this infinite filial love which I wish you to share.

THE FAITHFUL SOUL:

How wonderful it all is, O Jesus! But how shall I reproduce such filial love?

6

IV

My Mother, Your Mother

JESUS:

My brother, you cannot really reproduce My filial love toward Mary unless you are, as I am, her child. Do you know to what extent you are a child of Mary?

1. All the faithful think they know it, for they all call her their Mother. The greater number of them, however, have only a very imperfect idea of Mary's Motherhood in their regard.

Many love Mary *as if* she were their Mother: tell Me, what would your mother answer you, if you said to her, "I love you *as if* you were my mother?"

Many think that Mary is their Mother solely in virtue of the words I pronounced before I died, when, seeing My Mother standing at the foot of the Cross, and next to her My beloved disciple, I said to her, "Woman, behold thy son," and to John, "Behold thy Mother." My words could very well have confided a maternal mission to Mary and created dispositions in her resembling those of a mother. Yet, if her Motherhood had depended on these words alone, it would have been a mere adoptive Motherhood. Now, I want you to realize that Mary is your *true* Mother in the supernatural order, just as she who gave you birth is your *true* mother in the natural order.

2. A mother is one who gives life. Mary has given you life—the most real life.

7

She gave it to you at Nazareth, on Calvary, and in your Baptism.

At *Nazareth* she conceived you, in conceiving Me.

She knew that by answering the angel Gabriel "Yes" or "No," she would either give you life or leave you in death. She said "Yes" in order that you might live. By consenting to give Me life, she also consented to give it to you. In becoming My Mother, she became yours. From that moment, in the designs of God and in her own designs—for she had some idea of the designs of God and adhered to them with her whole heart—you constituted a part of My Mystical Body. I was the Head and you were a member. Mary bore us both, though in different ways, in her maternal womb; for the members and the Head have not a separate existence.

3. On *Calvary*, she brought you forth when she offered Me as a sacrifice for you.

Your deliverance from sin and death was only consummated on Golgotha. It was there that I "destroyed him who had the empire of death," and by My death merited for you the grace of living My life. Now, it was in union with Mary that I accomplished this work. She had conceived Me as a Victim; she had nourished and brought Me up for the Sacrifice, and at the supreme moment, she offered Me to the Father for your salvation and renounced in your favor her maternal rights over Me. And she who, ever Virgin, experienced only joy in the birth of her Firstborn Son, gave birth to you and your brothers amid the most agonizing sorrow.

4. At that moment, her Motherhood in your regard was consummated. That is why I then wanted to proclaim it by confiding John to Mary and Mary to John. My words did not create that motherhood; they attested, confirmed, and completed it at the most solemn hour of My life—the hour when My Mother, having become your Mother in the full sense of the word, was best able to understand her maternal mission.

5. At your *Baptism* Mary not only gave you the right to supernatural life as she did on Calvary, she actually brought you forth to it. As far as the supernatural world was concerned, your natural mother brought you forth a stillborn child. That you might come to life, Sanctifying Grace had to be infused into you at the baptismal font.

This Sanctifying Grace came to you through Mary, for, except through her no grace is ever given. When you were transformed from a child of wrath to a child of God, it was Mary who gave birth to you unto that life divine.

6. Do you understand now how Mary, by making you a participant of the life of God, is really your Mother in the supernatural order, just as the one who gave you human life is really your mother in the natural order?

Mary is even more truly your Mother.

She is more truly your Mother, first, because of the way in which she has given you life.

For your birth, she paid incomparably more than your earthly mother. That she might bring you forth to life, she offered the Eternal Father the unutterable sufferings and the very life of One who was infinitely dearer to her than her own life.

She continues during the whole course of your existence to busy herself with you, whereas earthly mothers care for their children only until they are adults. You will always be her "little child whom she continues to bear until Christ be formed in you." And if, unhappily, you should lose your supernatural life, she is not like earthly mothers who helplessly grieve and weep over the corpse of their child. She can restore life to you each time you may happen to lose it.

She loves you—you, all imperfect and ungrateful as you are; she loves you with a love which surpasses in intensity and in purity the motherly love of all the mothers in the world.

7. Above all, she is more truly your Mother because of the nature of the life which she has given to you.

It is not a passing life like your terrestrial one, but a life without end; not a life full of imperfections and anguish like your present existence, but a life incomparably happy; not a created life, human or angelical, but—and understand it well—a participation in uncreated life, in the very life of God, in the life of the Most Blessed Trinity. And that is why this life will be endless and incomparably happy, because it is a sharing in the eternity and in the beatitude of God. What human motherhood could compare with such a Motherhood?

Now, Mary is your true Mother, and so perfect a Mother, just because she is *My* Mother.

And you are My brother—My infinitely dear

brother—because My Father is your Father and My Mother is your Mother.

THE FAITHFUL SOUL:

No, Jesus, I did not know to what extent Mary was my Mother. How much nearer You have just brought her to me! Thanks, O Jesus, for that gift of gifts.

V

You Love Mary; Now Not You, But I Love Her in You

JESUS:

My brother, since My life is your life, and My Mother your Mother, it is easy for you to imitate My filial love toward her.

1. But you should not imitate Me only as a disciple imitates his master, or as a Christian on earth imitates his celestial patron. I am more than a model placed before you, I am, for you, an interior principle of life.

2. You live by Me. My dispositions must become your dispositions.

I am the vine, you are a branch. The same sap circulates in the stock of the vine as in the branches.

I am the head, you are a member of My Mystical Body; the selfsame blood flows in the head and in the members.

When you are pure, it is I who am pure in

you; when you are patient, it is I who am patient in you; when you practice charity, it is I who practice charity in you. You live; it is no longer you who live, it is I who live in you. You love My Mother; no, it is no longer you who love her, it is I who love her in you.

Do you understand now why you are so happy in loving Mary? It is I in you who am happy in loving her.

3. You participate in My life, but My life is far from being perfect in you. If it were perfect, you would think, you would feel, you would will, you would act in all things as I do.

There are too many obstacles to the free unfolding of My activity in your soul. Too often I live in your soul as a prisoner lives in his cell.

You must remove these obstacles; by generous efforts you must succeed in thinking My thoughts, in willing as I will. You must fill up what is lacking of My life in you.

You share in My filial love toward My Mother, but My filial love toward her is far from being perfect in you.

You must remove the obstacles; by generous effort you must succeed in acquiring My thoughts, My sentiments, My desires, My will, My activity in regard to My Mother.

You must fill up what is lacking in you of My filial love toward My Mother.

4. Do you begin to catch a glimpse of what I am trying to reveal to you about your devotion to Mary?

You should love My Mother because I love her;

you should love her in the way I love her; you should love her with the selfsame love as I do.

THE FAITHFUL SOUL:

> *O Jesu dulcis, O Jesu pie,*
> *O Jesu, fili Mariae.*

> O sweet Jesus, O loving Jesus,
> O Jesus, Son of Mary.

PART 2—JESUS SETS FORTH THE REQUIREMENTS OF THE IDEAL

JESUS:

My brother, I have shown you the ideal; I am now going to show you what it requires.

You have followed Me with joy up till now. Follow Me henceforth with joy still, but above all with love and generosity.

It is no longer a matter of merely contemplating and admiring your Model; the question now is how to reproduce His characteristic traits.

I am going to indicate them to you one by one. But you will reproduce them only very imperfectly unless you have learned to deny yourself and to love.

I

To Imitate Me, Give Yourself to My Mother without Reserve

JESUS:

By becoming the Son of Mary, I gave Myself entirely to her.

1. Creator and Sovereign Master of all things, I willed, out of love, to belong to Mary and to depend upon her. I willed to belong to her by the most intimate ties there are, the ties of blood, which nothing can dissolve.

From all eternity I chose this filial dependence on Mary and, from the first instant of My Incarnation in the bosom of Mary, I ratified with My human will that decree of My eternal love and took ineffable delight in it.

As the Son of a Virgin, I belonged to My Mother as no other child ever belonged to his; and, as no other child could possibly do, I willed to perpetuate this state of total dependence.

I did not leave My Mother as do those sons who go to found a family; I stayed with her until the moment appointed for the accomplishment of My public mission. And even afterwards, up to the very moment of My supreme Sacrifice, I remained in perfect conformity with My Mother's will, because she never had any other will than that of My Eternal Father.

More than that: in Heaven itself I keep in mind and will always keep in mind that I am her Son. And, although it is I who reign and command there, I will always yield to all her maternal desires with perfect filial love.

2. Following My example, give yourself as a well-beloved child to My Mother entirely, unreservedly, and forever.

Give her your body and its manifold activities, your soul and all its powers.

Give her all your possessions, material and

spiritual, natural and supernatural.

Give her all that you are and all that you will be, all that you have and all that you will have, all that you do and all that you will do. Let there be no interior or exterior possession of yours which does not belong to her.

3. Do not be satisfied with giving yourself to Mary just to become her property. She wants to use you, not as an inert object, but as a beloved son who assists his mother. For, as she will reveal to you later, I have confided to her a great mission in the world; and, to accomplish this mission, she wishes to depend upon you.

4. Give yourself without any idea of recompense. Not out of personal interest, nor with a view to receiving more in return, nor for the consolation you experience in thus giving yourself; but out of pure filial love, just as I have given Myself to her.

You will have consolations, but you will also experience trials: be not anxious about either, for your Mother will take care of them. Your role is merely to think of giving yourself totally and lovingly.

5. Give yourself forever.

There are many who, in a moment of fervor, have professed to give all to My Mother, but there are almost as many who, after giving all in a general way, have taken everything back little by little.

In the hour of trial, when their total donation demanded sacrifices, they said, "This is a hard saying, and who can hear it?" And they ceased walking in the way of their entire consecration.

Will you do as they? It requires heroism sometimes to live up to your total consecration to Mary, for you must climb with My Mother even to the summit of Calvary. Do you feel yourself capable of such heroism?

6. Acquire the habit of frequently renewing your consecration to your heavenly Mother.

Renew it at your waking hour so that your whole day may belong to her.

Renew it when you receive Me in Holy Communion. At that moment when you are but one with Me, give yourself anew to My Mother as her well-beloved child.

Renew it at three o'clock in the afternoon in memory of that solemn hour when Mary offered Me as a Sacrifice to God and thus gave birth to you and heard Me proclaim: "Woman, behold thy son."

Renew it before your principal actions, in order to recall to mind that it is not for yourself that you ought to act but solely for her.

Renew it especially in the trials of life. Say to her then, "O Mother, when I gave myself wholly to you in the enthusiasm of my filial love, I did not foresee this sacrifice. But I did intend to give myself entirely, and I do not want to retract my donation. Whatever you wish, because you wish it, cost what it may!"

7. Do you want to become generous enough always to live your donation to the very limit? Do not stop to consider the sacrifice. Just consider Myself and My Mother. Love will stimulate you and

My grace will sustain you.

And if you feel your courage weakening, pray. Will not your Mother always come to the aid of her child when you call on her to keep you faithful? Will not your Elder Brother give you the strength to tend toward the ideal to which He Himself has called you?

THE FAITHFUL SOUL:

> I am all thine, dear Mother,
> And all I have belongs to thee.[1]

II

To Imitate Me, Love My Mother

1. *The Reason*

JESUS:

My brother, it is love which has made Me the Son of Mary. Everything in My relations with her is explained by love. If you wish to understand My filial piety toward her, you must above all understand My love for her.

1. How I long to communicate to you a little of that love for My Mother which burns in My Heart. Strive to make yourself pure, humble, and generous, that I may pour into your heart the greatest possible amount of My filial love.

2. In recollection and prayer, ponder over all

---

1. See page 105 for a method of consecration to Mary.

that I have thus far let you glimpse of My love for Mary: how I chose her from all eternity and overwhelmed her with privileges; how I lived intimately with her and associated her in My mission; how I love her, and will forever continue to love her through the Saints and through the whole Church on earth and in Heaven.

3. Then, entering more deeply into My Heart, meditate upon the motives which have impelled Me to love her so much.

I have loved her and I now love her because she is My Mother, a Mother of ravishing beauty and perfection; a Mother who gave Me more joy by the least of her words, by the least of her glances, than all the Saints ever gave Me by their most heroic actions; a Mother who loves Me far more than do the angels and the blessed in Heaven; a Mother who lived only for Me and who accepted in all willingness the most excruciating martyrdom a creature has ever endured.

4. I have loved her because she aided Me in fulfilling the mission confided to Me by My Father;—because she gave Me My human nature so that I could preach the Good Tidings to men and die for them;

—because in this mission she united herself to me by an act of her will, by her supplications, her sacrifices, and by her presence at the foot of My Cross;

—because she will labor even to the end of time to convert sinners, to sanctify the just, and to lead numberless souls to Me;

—because she herself is the great triumph of

My mission as Redeemer, and because, by redeeming her in such a perfect manner, I have done more than by redeeming all the rest of the world.

5. I have loved her and I love her—because, thanks to her, I was able as man to offer to My Father adoration, reparation, and glory of infinite value—something I could not have given Him without the humanity with which she clothed Me;

—because she united herself to Me in My homage to the Father, and adored, venerated, and loved Him as He has never been adored, venerated, and loved by all the Saints and angels united;

—and because, through her, men will understand My Father better and act more and more His dutiful sons.

6. Never cease meditating upon the immensity of My love for My Mother; you will never reach its limits, not even during all eternity.

As you meditate upon it, put yourself in My place; become Jesus, the Firstborn Son of Mary—for really My life is your life—and try to feel what I felt.

7. Consider, too, the special love that Mary has for you.

She loves you because I have loved you even to the point of dying for you, and because she loves what I love.

She loves you because your mother loves that child most who has cost her most pain, and you have cost her indescribable sufferings.

She loves you because, in order to bring you forth to life, she had to give Me up to death.

She loves you because you and I are one, and

because in loving you she loves Me.

THE FAITHFUL SOUL:

O Jesus, I loved Mary when I still understood only vaguely what she is to me. Now that I begin to understand how really she is my mother, how much You love her, and how much she loves me, could I do otherwise than love her with all the powers of my being?

III

To Imitate Me, Love My Mother

2. *The Way*

JESUS:

My brother, do you really love her whom I love so much, and who loves you so much?

1. You believe you do, for you feel joy when you speak to her and enthusiasm when you sing her praises. But on earth love does not mean joy and enthusiasm principally but rather work and suffering.

2. If you love Mary, you will want to work for her.

You will be glad to give her your activity, your time, your efforts. No labor will be too painful for you when there is question of her glory, no enterprise will seem impossible for you when there is question of promoting her interests.

The day when you find some Marian task beyond

your strength, tell yourself that you have ceased to love her!

Now, My Mother does reserve a task for you, a very noble, and at times a very difficult one.

3. If you love Mary you will want to suffer for her.

He who no longer loves Mary when he must suffer for her has never truly loved her; he has merely loved himself in the consolations she has given him.

Do not refuse to suffer, for you would be refusing to love.

Do not merely accept suffering; love it. Are you not glad to be able to show your love? Are you not glad to be able to love more?

4. In order to learn how to love always more and more, put into practice the four means which I am going to indicate to you:

a) Apply yourself to accomplish your thousand little daily duties and sacrifices with the greatest possible love. If you succeed in never saying "No" to your Mother in little things, you will never say "No" to her in great things.

b) Do not cease to study your Mother.

Learn from books all that you can about her privileges, her mission, her life, and the lives of those who have loved and served her. Then reflect on what you have learned.

You will never finish studying her because you will never finish understanding what I have done for her and what she has done for Me and for you.

c) Live constantly in union with her. You cannot live in intimacy with her without finding her more lovable and without loving her more day by day. I shall explain to you later how you can live always united to her, in imitation of Me.

d) Finally, ask of Me the grace of loving her and of growing constantly in this love.

The love of My Mother is a grace—a choice grace. But grace is obtained by prayer: "Ask and you shall receive."

Ask without hesitating, for this grace cannot fail to be conformable to My designs.

To hesitate would be to blaspheme My Mother and Myself; it would amount to supposing that I am able not to want you to love her.

Is not your very desire of loving her due to My inspiration? Would I have inspired such a desire, if I did not wish to satisfy it?

Ask for this grace every day.

Ask for it above all when I come and unite Myself to you in the Holy Eucharist.

At that moment I come to you as Mary's Son, clothed in the human nature which I received from her and by which I make you participate in My divinity.

"He that eateth Me, the same also shall live by Me." To love My Mother with the same love as I bear her, is not *that* living by Me?

It is especially in Holy Communion that I cause the love of My Mother to pass from My heart into yours; there, especially, it is no longer you who live, it is I who live in you; and it is no longer you who love Mary, it is I who love her in you.

Hitherto, you have hardly ever asked Me for this grace; ask and you shall receive, that your joy may be full.

O good Jesus, by the love with which Thou lovest Thy Mother, grant me, I beseech Thee, to love her truly, as Thou truly lovest her and wishest her to be loved.—*Saint Anselm.*

IV

To Imitate Me, Obey My Mother

JESUS:

My brother, do you wish to manifest your love for My Mother as I manifested Mine? Be obedient, then, as I was.

1. As a little Baby, I let her do with Me what she wished. I allowed Myself to be put in the crib, carried in her arms, nursed and dressed by her, taken by her to Jerusalem, to Egypt, to Nazareth.

As soon as I had sufficient strength, I showed Myself eager to fulfill her desires and even to anticipate them.

After astonishing the doctors in the Temple, I returned to Nazareth with her and was subject to her.

Until the age of thirty years I stayed with her and always deferred to her least wishes.

2. I found unspeakable happiness in obeying her. By My obedience, I repaid her for all she did for Me, and above all for what she would one day have to suffer for Me.

3. I obeyed her in all simplicity, for, although I was her God, I was also her Son; she was My Mother and the representative of My Father.

In all simplicity, she gave Me commands, directed Me—ineffably happy to see Me attentive to her smallest wishes.

Do you wish to cause her this happiness again? Obey her then as I did.

4. My Mother has orders to give you. She commands you first of all by the voice of duty.

Some make their devotion to Mary consist in pictures and statues, in candles and flowers; others, in formulas of prayer and in hymns; others, in sentiments of tenderness and enthusiasm; others, in practices and sacrifices over and above the demands of duty.

There are some who believe they love her very much because they rejoice in talking to her, or because they see themselves, in imagination, accomplishing great things for her, or because they endeavor constantly to think of her.

All these things are good, but they are not the essential. "Not every one that saith to Me, Lord, Lord, shall enter into the kingdom of heaven; but he that doth the will of My Father who is in heaven, he shall enter into the kingdom of heaven."

Likewise, it is not those who say, "Mother! Mother!" who are the true children of Mary, but those who always do her will.

Now Mary has no other will than Mine, and My will in your regard is the accomplishment of your duty.

5. Strive therefore, above all, to do your duty and to do it out of love for her: your duty, great or small, easy or painful, interesting or monotonous, glorious or obscure.

With a view to pleasing your Mother, be more docile toward your superiors, more amiable toward your equals, more gentle with your inferiors, more kind to all. Be more punctual in your obedience, more conscientious in your work, more patient in your trials.

6. But accomplish all this with a maximum of love and with a pleasant smile.

Look cheerfully at your painful task, your prosaic occupations, the monotonous succession of your obligations; or rather, look with a smile at your Mother who asks you to accomplish your duty in high spirits that you may prove your love for her.

7. It is relatively easy for you to see the will of Mary in what God commands you to do. But how hard it is for you to see it in what God allows to happen.

Yet the God of love allows things to happen only out of love, and He always has His Mother cooperate in His loving plans in your behalf.

So, then, when things or men make you suffer, do not think of them, but think of your Mother, who by these things or men is striving to make you more pure and more happy. Say to her: "Behold the son of the handmaid of the Lord; be it done unto me according to thy word!"

8. Mary sends you still other indications of her will: the inspirations of grace.

Every grace comes to you through her.

When grace solicits you to renounce a certain pleasure, to curb this tendency, to make good that fault or negligence, to practice that act of virtue, it is Mary who is sweetly and lovingly manifesting her desires to you.

Sometimes you take alarm at the exigencies of these inspirations. Have no fear; it is your Mother who is speaking to you, your Mother who desires your happiness.

Recognize her voice, trust her love, and answer "Yes" to all she demands of you.

9. There is a fourth way for you to practice obedience toward Mary; it is to carry out the special task that she is going to confide to you. Be ready!

THE FAITHFUL SOUL:

O Jesus, I am beginning to understand: my whole program will consist in practicing what the Holy Spirit has said of You: "He was subject to them."

V

To Imitate Me, Honor My Mother

JESUS:

My brother, I am the God before whom the angels veil their faces, whom they tremblingly adore. Nevertheless, I humbly honored Mary, for although I am God, I am also her Son!

1. It is I who gave the commandment, "Honor thy father and thy mother." How could I do otherwise than keep this commandment Myself

in all its perfection?

2. I have honored Mary because she is My Mother—a Mother incomparably holy and august, the representative of My Heavenly Father. Imagine, if you can, with what profound and tender respect I acted in her presence, greeted her, listened to her, spoke with her, and carried out her every wish when I was a Child, an Adolescent, or a Man.

How extremely happy she appeared at these marks of honor; she accepted them in all simplicity, because such was the will of the Father, and kept repeating to herself the while, "He hath regarded the humility of His handmaid; He hath exalted the humble."

3. To honor her, I have done immensely more than give her these marks of deference.

Was it not out of veneration for My Mother that I exempted her from the law of Original Sin, preserved her from concupiscence, surrounded her with so many safeguards that not the slightest breath ever tarnished the purity of her soul?

Was it not from a feeling of infinite respect that I willed to preserve the integrity of her body at My Conception and My Birth, and to transport that virginal body to Heaven before the corruption of the tomb could touch it?

Was it not to exalt My Mother all the more that, from the moment of her Immaculate Conception, I overwhelmed her with a superabundance of graces—graces superior to those of all other creatures united—that I associated her in My mission of Redemption and crowned her Queen of Heaven and earth?

And, as I have already told you, those marks of

honor which the Church, by the solemn teaching of her pastors or by the voice of an enthusiastic people, has not ceased to multiply from century to century, and will multiply still more in centuries to come—what are they if not a partial realization of My desire to honor Mary?

4. "Behold," she cried one day under the impulse of the Holy Spirit, "all generations shall call me blessed." Her prophecy must be accomplished; over the whole globe the name of My Father must be hallowed and the name of My Mother glorified!

5. In order to honor Mary as I have honored her, and as I wish her to be honored, begin by understanding her better.

Do not cease contemplating her dignity, her privileges, her perfection, her mission.

Then humble yourself in your nothingness and misery. The more you belittle yourself in your own eyes, the greater will be your capacity for understanding the grandeur of My Mother.

Above all, take into your soul the dispositions of My soul: look at Mary with My eyes, admire her with My mind, rejoice in her beauty with My heart.

6. Honor her by your eagerness to take part in public prayers and feasts in her honor.

Honor her by some practices of piety which you will faithfully offer her every day, by the sacrifices you make in order to aid in her glorification.

Honor her by making her known and loved round about you, by uniting yourself with other privileged sons of Mary, so as to serve her with them.

Honor her by giving yourself to her, by fighting for her and under her direction. The way? She will reveal that to you later.

Honor her above all by your conduct. Become a saint and you will thereby do more for her honor than if, while remaining a mediocre Christian, you composed learned books about her.

7. Honor her in My name and in your own name. Honor her for those who do not honor her: for pagans who have no knowledge of her, for heretics who blaspheme her, for bad Christians who fail to pray to her, for the consecrated souls who show themselves lukewarm in her service.

8. Honor her to the limit of your power, for she is beyond all praise and you will never sufficiently praise her.

Honor her with no fear of excess. You will never honor her as much as I did, nor so much as I wish her to be honored.

THE FAITHFUL SOUL:

Blessed be the name of the Virgin Mary,
Now and forever!

VI

To Imitate Me, Resemble My Mother

JESUS:

My brother, children generally resemble their mother. I resembled Mine more than any child of man ever resembled his.

1. Born of her alone, My features, My looks, My walk, My gestures, My whole exterior, recalled My Virginal Mother. Whoever saw Me recognized

Me at once as the Son of Mary.

Greater still than our physical resemblance was the resemblance between our souls. My Heavenly Father had modeled Mary according to My likeness in order that like a true Mother she might form Me according to her likeness. And by constantly applying herself to observe Me, to ponder in her heart all that I did and said, she succeeded in reproducing all My dispositions with incomparable perfection.

In every matter, we had therefore the same thoughts, the same sentiments, the same will. Her spirit had passed into Me and My spirit into her.

2. Strive to resemble My Mother as I resembled her.

Resemble her exteriorly by your modesty. When seeing you, may people experience something of the same reverence and calmness of spirit which they felt when looking upon My Mother.

3. Resemble her above all interiorly.

Copy her virtues. They are incomparably sublime and at the same time incomparably simple. For the life of Mary was similar to yours. It is easy for you to understand or to surmise how she acted or would have acted in your place.

Like her, begin by studying all virtues as they are found in Me. Then think of your Mother and see how she reproduced them. You will learn your lesson from Me, but you will understand it much better once your Mother has explained it to you.

4. Be pure, in order to be a worthy child of the Virgin of virgins.

Be humble and simple, forgetful of self, as was the Handmaid of the Lord.

Be recollected in God, and, like your Mother, ponder on all that has been revealed to you about Me.

Be strong in your faith, believing the Word of the Lord despite any appearances to the contrary, as she believed.

Be submissive to all that God wills, and know only one answer to give Him: "Behold the son of Thy handmaid, be it done unto me according to Thy word."

Be full of charity to your neighbor, devoting yourself to him as did Mary in the house of Elizabeth, at the wedding feast of Cana, and especially on Calvary.

Apply yourself to imitate in particular that one of My Mother's virtues which you lack most and which is most necessary for you.

5. Imitate not only her virtues but also her dispositions toward those who were nearest and dearest to her: toward her beloved parents, Joachim and Anne; toward John, My favorite disciple and My substitute with her; toward Joseph especially, her husband and My virginal foster father, toward whom she manifested unutterable affection, veneration, and gratitude for all that he was to Me and to her. You would not be her true child if you did not apply yourself to love and venerate one who was so dear to her.

6. Imitate, above all, her dispositions toward Me. Mary was created only for Me; she breathed, worked, and suffered only for Me.

From her you will learn to live for Me alone and to sacrifice yourself entirely for My cause.

And this you will learn quickly and perfectly, for the contemplation of My Mother's dispositions toward Me will exercise a singular power of attraction and transformation in you—a power made up at once of strength and of tenderness, of intelligence and of love, and also of a very special grace.

At her side, on account of that sympathy which exists between mother and child, you will experience what she experienced in My company. Will it be at all astonishing if, in her presence, you easily come to adopt My dispositions?

7. Following her example, you will also enter into closer relations with My Father, whose privileged daughter she knew herself to be from the moment of her Immaculate Conception, and with the Holy Spirit, who had chosen her for His infinitely beloved Spouse.

8. The imitation of My Mother will inspire you with still another disposition—that of immense love for souls. Of this she will speak to you herself.

THE FAITHFUL SOUL:

O Jesus, make me resemble Your Mother that she may make me resemble You.

VII

To Imitate Me, Have Confidence in My Mother

JESUS:

My brother, every child has confidence in its mother. I had supreme confidence in Mine.

1. I trusted in her for My material needs.

I feed the birds of the air and I clothe with their splendor the lilies of the field; but I wished to have the same material needs as all other children of men. I entrusted Myself to My Mother. She nourished Me, clothed Me, and took care of Me.

My life was menaced, I did not worry—My Mother carried Me into a strange country while I tranquilly slept in her arms.

2. I entrusted Myself to My Mother for the accomplishment of My mission.

Soon after I became Man, I wished to sanctify My precursor, to manifest Myself to the Jews and the Gentiles, to the aged Simeon and the Prophetess Anne. My Mother took care of it all.

In order to make reparation for Original Sin, I, the new Adam, willed to associate My Mother with Myself as the new Eve by a cooperation of will, of prayer, and of sacrifice. She understood perfectly, and generously consented.

3. I entrusted Myself to her in the agonies that this mission caused Me.

My soul was sorrowful beyond the power of man to conceive; sorrowful at the sight of the entirely material worship—often hypocritical—rendered to My Father; sorrowful because the multitudes did not understand Me, enemies opposed Me in bad faith, and even My friends were inconstant and had only earthly ideals; sorrowful above all because numberless souls were being lost, souls infinitely dear to Me, for whom I was going to shed My Blood in vain. I was sorrowful unto death even to the extent of asking My Father to let this chalice pass from Me.

And yet, I had an immense consolation: My Mother. *She* understood Me; *she* knew how to adore in spirit and in truth; *she* took part in My failures and in My anguish; *she* loved Me just so much more when the Pharisees hated and attacked Me, or when My disciples disappointed Me by their cowardice; *she* watched and prayed with Me during the whole time of My hidden life and likewise during the whole time of My public mission; *she* was at the foot of the Cross, steadily believing when everyone else was hesitating in his faith; in *her* My work of Redemption completely succeeded; *she* was My supreme triumph!

4. Follow My example and trust in My Mother. Have confidence—she is all powerful. Have I not made her the Distributrix of all graces? Is she not able to give all she wishes, to whom she wishes, and at any time she wishes?

Have confidence: she is goodness itself. Since I made her all-powerful, could I have failed to make her at the same time all-merciful?

Have confidence: I am her Child. What could I refuse My Mother?

Have confidence: you are her child. Does a mother ever refuse her child anything she can give to it?

Have confidence: you have given yourself entirely to her. Could she be less generous than you?

Have confidence: in giving to you, it is to Me that she gives, for she knows that I live in you and that whatever is done to the least of My brothers is done to Me. When you invoke her, you

36

give her the joy of continuing to take care of Me: to nourish, carry, shield, and rear Me.

Have confidence: she desires to give you more than you desire to receive, because she loves you more, and loves Me in you more than you can ever love yourself.

Have confidence: because you would grieve her by hesitating, because hesitation implies doubt of My Mother's love for you and for Me.

5. Why is it, then, that your confidence is not always unshakable?

You do not merit to be heard by her, you say, because of your lukewarmness in her service.

Your negligence is great, indeed, yet it will never be so great as your Mother's love for you.

You ought to have confidence not because *you* are good, but because *she* is good. Does she cease to be good when you are bad?

6. But you do not know whether your request is conformable to God's designs upon you, and so you hesitate.

Listen, I am going to teach you a way of praying which is always in accord with His designs, and which you can always use with unshaken confidence.

First of all, understand this very clearly:

a) Your Mother has loving intentions regarding all your needs.

b) Her intentions are always in conformity with the designs of God and they are always capable of realization.

c) They are always worth more than your own intentions, for Mary knows better than you just what you need, and she has greater ambitions for you than you have for yourself.

Every time you desire something, therefore, ask your Mother to make her intentions in the matter come true, and rest assured, infallibly so, that you will get either what you desire or something better; and that you will get it not according to your own narrow views, but according to those of her immense love.

THE FAITHFUL SOUL:

But then, Jesus, it will be wonderful!

Henceforth, in order to have a faith that can move mountains and to be heard even beyond my fondest hopes, it will be sufficient, in every need, to ask my Mother to make her intentions in my regard come true.

VIII

To Imitate Me, Live United with My Mother

JESUS:

I have yet another essential feature of My filial love for Mary to reveal to you: My life of union with her.

1. If for every child there is nothing sweeter than intimacy with its mother, how great were the joys which My intimacy with Mary afforded Me?

The joys of those nine months of ineffable union, when I and My Mother were but one, and when as a living tabernacle she always carried

Me about in her. For unlike other children, I knew My Mother from the first moment of My earthly existence and from that time on there was between her and Myself a continual exchange of thoughts and affection.

The joys of those thirty years of unparalleled intimacy at Bethlehem, in Egypt, at Nazareth, when she carried Me in her arms, saw Me at her side, spoke to Me with her eyes and lips... thirty long years alone with her and Joseph.

The joys no less profound of the last three years of My life when, misunderstood by the multitude, unsupported by My friends, furiously attacked by My enemies, I thought of her who in her little Nazareth home thought of Me, understood Me, loved Me, and offered to the Father incessant supplications and sacrifices for the success of My mission.

2. I was to know other joys—joys coming to me from the generosity of My Apostles, from the faith and the devotedness of many disciples, and from the vision of countless pure, simple, generous souls who, even to the end of time, would believe in My love and would give themselves entirely to Me. But all these joys combined never equaled the least of those which I found in that union between Myself and My Mother, in that fusion of our souls into one.

3. Now, My dear brother, I want you to share this union in order to share this joy.

Along with infinite consolation you will draw from it great facility in the practice of all the other manifestations of filial love which I have been teaching you.

Near Mary you will apply yourself quite instinctively to renew and to live your entire consecration to her. You will feel your filial love growing greater day by day; you will find it easy to obey all her desires, even the least; you will become skillful in divining the marks of veneration that will please her most; you will spontaneously put yourself to the task of imitating her virtues and her dispositions; you will experience an invincible confidence in her maternal goodness.

Near her, you will learn many things which I have not explained to you because your heart will divine them by itself.

4. Try, therefore, to imitate Me by entering into the closest possible intimacy with My Mother.

Unite yourself to her in prayer.

Be faithful to the daily renewal of your consecration to her, to the daily recitation of the beads—at least of a decade—and to the prayers that you have resolved to offer to her every day. Several times a day look up to her who is constantly looking down upon you, her child.

5. But as you pray to her, recall to mind that it is in My name that you are invoking her; that it is I who continue to honor and love My Mother with your heart and lips. You will feel a great difference in your dispositions of confidence and love according as you speak to My Mother in your own name alone, or in My name and in union with My Heart.

6. Even when you want to speak to the Father or to the Holy Spirit or to Me, start by uniting yourself to My Mother. If you are close to her, your recollection will be more profound, your faith

more solid, your confidence more complete, and your love more ardent; for the perfect dispositions of My Mother will be united with yours.

7. Have recourse to Mary especially when you receive Me in the Sacrament of love. Ask her to lend you her faith, her hope, her confidence, her charity. Ask her to give Me to you and to transform you into Myself.

8. Unite yourself to her in your actions.

I worked for My Mother and with My Mother. You should do the same.

Offer her every one of your occupations, but do not reduce that offering to a mere formula. Do nothing but what she wishes, because she wishes it, and as she wishes it.

Be on your guard lest your whims, your evil tendencies, your personal interests supplant your original intention. Above all, in the occupations which tend to absorb or trouble you, be careful to renounce all self-seeking, so that you may act only according to the intentions of Mary.

Learn, little by little, to renew your offering during the course of your actions, even if only by a look.

9. Unite yourself to her in all the emotions of your soul. Mary's Heart and Mine always beat in unison. My joys were her joys; My sorrows, her sorrows; My hopes, her hopes; My fears, her fears; My love, her love.

Tell your Mother about everything that disturbs or impresses you. She understands the turmoil in the depth of your heart; she understands what you yourself cannot understand.

Are you sad? Share your affliction with her and she will help you to endure it or will change it into joy.

Are you happy? Tell her your happiness and she will intensify and purify it.

Do you feel discouraged? Lay your fears and failures before her and she will obtain real success for you.

Have you been successful in an enterprise? Go and thank her for it and ask her to assure the fruits of your labor.

Are you unable to make a choice in the midst of your perplexities? Consult her; she will enlighten and guide you.

Are you without strength and willpower? Come closer to her and renew your energy.

10. Tell her not only your profound emotions but even the simple impressions and reflections which your ordinary occupations suggest. Does not a child act in that way with its Mother? And do you not believe I acted in that way when I was near My Mother?

11. In these incessant communications with Mary, you do not need many words. How often does it not happen that children let their mother know their feelings and their needs by just crying "Mother!" and then looking at her with pleading eyes. On such occasions a mother has a wonderful intuition of what is meant. Better than any other mother, Mary knew what I meant when I uttered her name or looked at her. And her look answered Mine. Oh, what infinite joy it was for her and for Me!

In order to tell Mary your needs or your feelings, say to her simply, "Mother!" and look at her a moment, putting into that name all you wish to tell her: a protestation of love, an offering of your work, a cry of distress, a word of gratitude, your joy or your sorrow. Your Mother will understand and answer as only she can.

Even when simply pronouncing the word *Mother*, be conscious of speaking in My name: you will give Mary infinitely more joy and she will lavish infinitely more love upon you, if she hears My voice through yours repeating "Mother!"

THE FAITHFUL SOUL:

O Jesus, grant me the grace of accomplishing what You have just explained to me. Truly it will be Heaven upon earth to live in such intimacy with Mary after Your example.

IX

Come and Listen to Your Mother

JESUS:

My brother, you are beginning to understand what I did for My Mother and what you should do after My example. You have not yet learned all she did for Me and all she wants to do for you.

She brought Me up just as every real mother rears her child, and she was associated with Me in My mission of Redemption.

She wishes to bring you up, in turn, and to

associate you in her mission of Co-Redemptrix.

But she herself is going to explain her plans. Listen to her with docility and obey her with love, even as I was subject to her with an infinite love.

THE FAITHFUL SOUL:

O Jesus, Son of God and Son of Mary, my Creator and my Brother, what return shall I make for all You have done for me? You know very well that I have nothing of my own but my weakness and my sins. With Your grace, however, I can give You what You expect from me: I want to be to Mary what You were; I want to allow You to continue loving her through me.

And you, O Mary, Mother of God and my Mother! You have chosen me as your child of predilection. With your help I shall be another Jesus toward you.

At present you want to instruct and direct me. Speak, Mother, your child is listening. Command me to do whatever you wish, and give me the grace to carry out your commands.

I

My Aim: To Transform You into Jesus

MARY:

My beloved child, to whom I gave birth when giving birth to Jesus, in whom I see Jesus, and whom I love with the same love I have for Him, my Firstborn Son has taught you to be a son to me as He Himself was. I am going to be a mother to you as I was to Him.

1. Like Him, you have given yourself entirely to me. But I do not wish to keep you for myself alone: it is for Jesus and for you—for Jesus in you and in others—that I have called you to be my child of predilection. You cannot as yet understand all that I am telling you, but you will understand little by little.

2. First of all, I wish to take care of your education as I did for my Son Jesus. You are my child because you are one with Him, and so I shall still be rearing Him when I rear you.

3. Rearing you means teaching you to live fully the life of Jesus; it means making you think, love,

45

will, speak, and act as He did; in a word, it means changing you into Him.

It means bringing about in you a transformation similar to the Transubstantiation which the priest operates in the Sacred Host: to the physical eye the host always appears as bread, but to the eye of faith it is Jesus! You also, exteriorly, will remain yourself, but interiorly, in a certain way you will be Jesus Himself.

4. Perhaps you think this ideal too sublime for you. Do not be dismayed: I have a thorough knowledge of the Model, and I know how to form souls to His likeness. All the Saints have become saints through me. What I have done for others, can I not do for you? Only let me carry out my plans; on your part be docile to my word.

5. I am going to point out certain practices to aid you in this transformation. Apply yourself successively to them, and do not pass to the next until you have made a habit of the preceding one. Yet once you have adopted a practice, never give it up.

THE FAITHFUL SOUL:

O my Mother—I— become a saint! I, wretched sinner, so blameworthy in the past, so lukewarm at present, so inconstant, I fear, in the future. ... But I surrender myself to you. You can work any miracle, you can even make me a saint. Obtain for me the grace of never resisting your wishes.

II

Learn to Think the Thoughts of Jesus

1. *In Books*

MARY:

My child, in order to learn to live the life of Jesus, you must first learn to think the thoughts of Jesus.

1. The world thinks one way but Jesus thinks quite differently. Your thoughts are often nearer to those of the world than to those of Jesus.

2. The thoughts of Jesus are found in the Gospel and also in the books written by authors filled with the spirit of the Gospel. It is there, first of all, that you must study the thoughts of Jesus.

Reserve some moments of the day for devotional reading. Can you not find a quarter of an hour, or five minutes at least, each day? You find time for a host of other occupations much less necessary.

However short it may have to be, never omit your daily reading.

Fix upon the moment when you will do it, whether it be at the beginning, at the middle, or at the end of the day. Be punctual in starting at the time determined.

3. When opening your book, ask me to help you understand what Jesus is going to teach you, and in the course of your reading tell me the reflections it suggests to you.

While you read, keep in mind that it is Jesus who is speaking to you.

Read respectfully, to do honor to the words of Jesus.

Read slowly, not rushing on just to satisfy your curiosity, but trying to grasp the spirit of Jesus and how to live His life.

Apply your reading to your life. See which of your ideas or actions have to be reformed, and finish your reading with a resolution confided to me.

III

Learn to Think the Thoughts of Jesus

2. *By Direct Contact with Him*

MARY:

My child, there is another way of coming to think the thoughts of Jesus, a very rapid, sure, and efficacious way. It consists in putting yourself in direct contact with Him.

1. Contemplate Jesus, preferably in the Gospels.

Listen to His word, observe His action. But do not stop at the exterior; penetrate into His soul and discover behind His words and actions what He really thought and felt and willed.

See above all how with Him each word, each action proceeds from love. Jesus is more than a Teacher uttering words of wisdom. He is the God of love. You have not yet understood His teaching if you have not discovered its source: the infinite love of His Heart.

2. From the contemplation of Jesus, turn for a moment to the contemplation of yourself. Find out how far you are from thinking, feeling, willing as He does.

See what you must do, what obstacles you must avoid, what means you must take, what sacrifices you must impose upon yourself to bring about your transformation into Him.

3. While thus contemplating Jesus and comparing your conduct with His, speak to Him.

Speak to Him as if you saw Him. Is He not in you? Does He not hear your voice as truly as He formerly heard St. Peter's, St. Mary Magdalen's, and St. John's? Does He not love you as He loved His disciples; you especially, whom He has given to me to be, like John, my child of predilection?

Speak to Him directly, without any set formula of prayer. Tell Him in all simplicity what you are thinking, what you are feeling, and what you desire, just as you would speak about it to a brother or an intimate friend.

4. Do not forget to unite yourself to me in these intimate conversations with Jesus. You know that I am always near you and that to reach the Son you must go by way of the Mother.

As you yourself will find out, you will be less recollected, less at ease, less loving with Him, when you do not feel me near you.

I spent my life pondering over the things I saw and heard about my Son. Any meditation you make on Him will be but the repetition of one that I made centuries ago. Come close to me and

I will make you understand and feel what I understood and felt when I explored the deep mysteries of Jesus.

5. Do not seek to multiply thoughts and reasonings. Just believe, love and pray.

Believe! If Jesus said such or such a thing, the matter is settled. You need not look for other proofs. He said, so therefore it is true, infallibly true. Only believe.

Men about you may affirm the contrary, at least by their conduct. What does it matter? Jesus has said it; believe it! Men will pass away, but the Truth of Our Lord will remain forever.

Your feelings will incline you to side with men, or, at least, to remain indifferent to the teachings of Jesus. What does it matter? The question is not one of feeling but of believing. Jesus has said so! You must believe Him!

Unite yourself to me and you will believe with a purer and firmer faith.

Multiply your acts of faith. Multiply them, not as an effort at auto-suggestion, but in order to make Divine Truth penetrate to the depths of your soul, and to bring its practical consequences home to you clearly.

6. Love! Love the Truth, because Jesus loved it; love it because it was only out of love that He taught it to men.

Above all, love Jesus and learn to love Him more and more. According as you love Him more, you will imitate all the dispositions of His soul more perfectly, even without explicitly trying to do so.

Come to me and I will unite my love to yours,

and together we will love Jesus with a love incomparably pure and strong.

7. Pray! Ask Jesus to come and help your unbelief. Ask Him to make His thoughts, feelings, and wishes your own.

Ask me to reveal Jesus to you, and to make you live His life.

8. Among the dispositions of Christ, preferably study the one you lack most, or the one for which you experience a special attraction, or the one which a recent disturbing event proves you need at once.

9. Instead of seeking inspiration for your prayer in the Gospels, you may have recourse to some other religious book, or to a known formula of prayer, or to a sacred hymn. But endeavor to connect everything with Jesus; to believe, to love, and to practice everything for the sake of Jesus.

10. Prepare your conversation with Jesus by foreseeing what you intend to say to Him and by endeavoring to be more composed.

Always begin by asking me to lead you to my Son; put yourself in my presence, and then together we shall put ourselves in His.

End your conversation by taking a practical resolution in the way I shall teach you later.

11. From time to time throughout the day, when going to and fro, or in the intervals between your different occupations, try to recall the thought which most impressed you in your conversation with Jesus, and repeat acts of faith about it.

12. Do you now begin to understand the truth of what I was saying a few minutes ago about

the importance of this practice for anyone who wants to learn to think the thoughts of Jesus?

If so, you will also understand that you should never, for any reason, omit this daily conversation with Him.

Determine the precise moment when you are going to apply yourself to it and the length of time you will give to it; then, no matter what happens, hold to your decision.

Shorten it if necessary, but never omit it!

Do not omit it under the pretext that you have only time enough to say your morning and evening prayers. Rather reduce the length of these prayers by half in order to find a few moments for conversation with Jesus.

Do not omit it because the only time you have is already consecrated to the reception of Holy Communion. Receive Holy Communion, but make your preparation and thanksgiving by way of conversation with Jesus.

Do not omit it, objecting that otherwise you cannot do your spiritual reading. Make use of your reading as a preparation for your conversation, but always reserve some moments for direct contact with Jesus.

Do not omit it on account of the multiplicity of your occupations; the more occupations you have, the greater is your need of self-possession, and self-possession is best found in contact with God. The men who have done the most fruitful work are those who were most closely united to Jesus.

Do not omit it because you have been negligent

or unfaithful, or because you find yourself without thought or feeling. Who will cleanse you, who will cure you, if not Jesus? Come with me close to Him.

13. Have you understood me, my child? Either you will apply yourself resolutely and perseveringly to the practice I have just taught you and then it will be easy for me to transform you into Jesus, or like so many others you will not have the courage to do so, and then you will remain mediocre, and I will not be able to use you for the task I have reserved for you. Make your choice.

THE FAITHFUL SOUL:

O my Mother, I give you my word of honor, that never, under any pretext whatsoever, will I omit my daily chat with you and Jesus. Under your guidance I will apply myself constantly to study your Son.

IV

The Great Enemy of Jesus in You

MARY:

My child, knowing the thoughts of Jesus is not sufficient to make you immediately begin to live His life. You must at the same time fight and conquer the enemies who are opposed to the life of Jesus in you.

1. Now, the most dangerous of these enemies is yourself.

You would like to live only for Jesus and at the same time you would like to follow the tendencies of your depraved nature. Do not deceive yourself. "You cannot serve two masters." As long as your evil tendencies rule, Jesus cannot rule over you.

There must be no truce, no respite, no quarter in the war against your natural tendencies until they leave the stronghold to Jesus.

2. These are hard conditions, but you cannot escape them.

What a large number of my children I have seen who were once pious and generous, prepared to become saints and to exercise about them a compelling influence for good! Alas, because they were not able to recognize and combat their corrupt nature, they remained mediocre and failed to realize even a hundredth part of the good they were called to do, if, indeed, they were not miserably lost, dragging along in their fall a multitude of other souls.

3. Learn, therefore, to know the perverted tendencies of your nature. They are legion, for your body and soul in all their activities have been vitiated by Original Sin and weakened by the evil habits you have personally contracted or inherited from your ancestors.

Still, do not be embarrassed by the multiplicity of your enemies. They all obey a leader, and once he is conquered, all the others will, by the very fact, be crushed or reduced to relative impotence. It is your ruling passion which you must know above all. What is it?

4. Vanity? Are you in love with compliments, happy to receive them even if they are unmerited? Do you catch yourself dreaming about marvelous deeds calculated to attract the applause of men?

5. Pride? Have you an exaggerated idea of your worth and do you at times despise others? Do you treat others with haughtiness, harshness, or anger, especially those who do not bow to your superiority?

6. Touchiness? Do you become irritated at real or supposed criticism? At a lack of consideration, though it be involuntary? Are you easily offended? Do you find it hard to pardon? Are you tempted to give up a good work because someone has crossed you?

7. Ambition? Do you seek to put yourself forward? Is it your own glory or the glory of Christ that you seek? Are you one of those who devote themselves to a good cause only when they can be leaders in it, but who retire as soon as they must serve in the ranks?

8. Envy? Can you not stand having others succeed as well as you? Do you rejoice when they have failed?

9. Inconstancy? Are you the plaything of your feelings: at times enthusiastically ready for any sacrifice, then again depressed to the extent of being indifferent to everything? Do you start a multitude of enterprises without ever finishing any of them?

10. Light-mindedness? Do you give yourself too easily to exterior things? Do you find it difficult to recollect yourself and to give to serious matters the attention they merit?

11. Sensuality? Do you flatter your body? Are you always preoccupied about giving it all the satisfaction it craves in food, drink, repose, and, perhaps, in its still lower tendencies?

12. Laziness? Are you afraid of making an effort? Do you neglect your work? Do you retreat before the least sacrifice?

13. Egoism? Do you think only of yourself? Do you realize that others also have rights and that, if need be, you should suffer rather than have others suffer?

14. On examining yourself in this way, you will discover indications of a great number of these inordinate tendencies. No doubt you have the germs of all evil tendencies, but not all of them are predominant.

Which seems strongest and most pernicious? Which is the most ordinary cause of your disappointments, of your preoccupations, of your bad humor, of your joys?

When you catch yourself dreaming, is it a thought of vanity, vengeance, or sensuality that is occupying you?

Whence come the distractions that please you most, or that are the most difficult to banish?

With what have you been reproached by your parents, teachers, friends, or persons you have irritated?

About which of your tendencies would you say, "If I were not this way or that, I would get along much better with God and with men?"

15. Be very sincere in your examination and pray for light from Heaven, for it is easy to make a

mistake in this matter and to take for the predominant fault one which is more apparent but less deep-seated, or one which is rather easy to give up. Men are strongly attached to their predominant fault, because it is a companion who was born and reared with them, who has always lived with them, and who has constantly procured them satisfaction. Sometimes they even mistake it for their predominant good quality. Doubtless, everyone loves himself a great deal, but we must have the courage to love Jesus more.

Dare to recognize in all simplicity how much of yourself you must sacrifice for Him.

Do not fear. By renouncing a vain idol, you will possess the true God; by dying to your corrupt nature, you will live the life of Jesus.

THE FAITHFUL SOUL:

May Jesus reign, no matter how much it costs me! "He must increase, I must decrease."

V

"Put Ye On the Lord Jesus Christ"

MARY:

My child, it is a difficult task to recognize your great enemy; it is a task a thousand times greater to exterminate it. By yourself you will never succeed; but if you remain close to me, you will triumph.

1. Begin by carefully observing how your dominant tendency shows itself. Learn to recognize

the multiple forms, apparent or hidden, which it assumes, the circumstances in which it causes you the greatest harm.

2. Then start a relentless fight against it.

In this battle against your defects you can follow a twofold strategy:

Certain people bring all their energy to bear upon watching the diverse manifestations of their defects, so that they can note them down, count them, compare them, and endeavor each day to reduce their number.

This strategy will certainly produce good results if it is used with perseverance.

But this strategy if followed alone runs the risk of becoming tedious, and of being at times fraught with painful surprises. For, after having interrupted for some time your continual watchfulness over one fault in order to work at another point in your spiritual life, you will often notice that the original tendency is still there, quite as lively as before, though perhaps appearing in a slightly different guise. You occupied yourself with cutting away the weeds as they grew, but, having failed to tear them out by the roots and to replace the cockle by useful grain, you discover them springing up again just as thickly as before.

3. I am going to teach you an easier and more efficacious strategy; one which, if it does not replace the other altogether, can at least complete it.

Study in Jesus the virtue directly opposed to your predominant tendency. Are you proud? Consider His humility. Are you irritable? Contemplate His sweetness. Are you selfish? Admire His forgetfulness of self and His readiness to sacrifice Himself for sinners. Are you sensual-minded? Meditate on His Passion.

4. Make use of your daily talks with Jesus in order to study in Him the disposition which you lack. See what Jesus thought, felt, said, and did. Set your heart on this disposition of Jesus, your Model; fill yourself with enthusiasm for it.

Then compare it with your own disposition.

Ask Jesus, and ask me, to change you into Him.

Then plan how you will live this disposition of Jesus during the day; that is: 1) on the basis of your experience of the morning or previous day, foresee the occasions when you will be likely to give in to your defect; 2) decide on definite times when you will repeat acts of faith and various invocations tending to establish in your soul the disposition of Jesus that you wish to acquire.

Always submit each and every one of your resolutions to me. Otherwise they will risk being vague and ineffectual.

In your Sacramental and Spiritual Communions, ask Jesus to make you live of His life.

5. Throughout the day, recall the thought of Jesus, meek, humble, patient—according to the disposition of His soul you wish to reproduce.

You should recall it in particular at those moments when your evil tendency seeks to reassert itself. Instead of making painful efforts to resist it, look peacefully at your Model and say, "Jesus, what would You think, what would You do if You were in my place? Come and make me live Your life." And Jesus will command the sea and the waves, and over your soul there will come a great calm.

6. By dint of contemplating Jesus and of drawing Him unto yourself by your prayers, you will gradually succeed in detaching yourself from that tendency to which you cling so strongly, and you will begin to have no other dispositions than those of Jesus.

Still, distrust that enemy; he may take you by surprise even at the moment you think yourself perfectly secure. Examine yourself from time to time, be it merely by a rapid glance, and see whether he is not trying to come to life under a new form.

7. My Son has instructed you to imitate your Mother. After observing the dispositions of Jesus, look at my own. When you try to imagine what I probably thought, felt, or did, or what I would do in your place in regard to some fault that you ought to overcome or some virtue that you ought to acquire, it is still Jesus whom you are learning to know better and to reproduce more perfectly.

THE FAITHFUL SOUL:

O Mary, teach Jesus to me, that I may live only His life!

VI

Three Means of Success

MARY:

My child, in order to push forward more quickly the work of transforming yourself into Jesus, you must proceed methodically. I am going to teach you three means that can be of great help in that task.

Daily Examination:

1. Every day find a moment, preferably toward the middle of the day, when you will examine briefly how your spiritual work is getting on.

Find out what you have done since the beginning of the day to live the life of Jesus as regards such or such a disposition of His, and then determine what you are going to do during the rest of the day.

In the evening before going to bed, cast a glance back over the day to see what you will have to avoid or do in order to improve matters on the morrow.

2. Carefully note the two following points:

First, as I have already explained, apply yourself less to counting your faults than to determining what Jesus would have thought, felt, and done in your place under the various circumstances in which your corrupt nature has again asserted itself; and foresee how you will imitate His dispositions the next time these same circumstances appear.

Secondly, make this examination in the form of a conversation with Jesus and with me. In this manner you will succeed much better than if you make a dry inquiry into your spiritual work all by yourself. Tell Us where you succeeded and where you failed; submit your resolutions to Us, and ask Us to help you live the life of Jesus more fully.

Spiritual Renewals:

3. Here is a second means, that will considerably hasten the work of identifying yourself with Jesus.

Arrange for yourself throughout the day a certain number of brief pauses, one or two in the morning and as many in the afternoon, according as your occupations permit.

At these moments, first enter into close contact with Jesus and with me again, even if it were by simply repeating His name and mine slowly and with great confidence and love.

After this, cast a rapid glance over what you have done in the way of imitating Jesus since the previous renewal and foresee what you will do until the following one.

Thus you will keep yourself spiritually active, and your union with Jesus and me will become closer and closer.

Retreats:

4. Finally, at certain intervals, you must devote more time to the interests of your soul.

Each year, endeavor to make a few days of retreat, or at least employ the free moments of several days in closer intimacy with Jesus and me. During that time think over once more the instructions We have given you; examine yourself to discover why you have not made more headway during the past year, and how you will make more progress during the coming year.

5. Every month, preferably the first Saturday or Sunday, recollect yourself during a part of your

free time in order to consider in my presence just where you are with your spiritual work, and in order to take more efficacious resolutions for the new month.

6. Every week on a determined day find a few minutes to review with me your efforts of the past week and to prepare those of the week to come.

7. Fidelity to such a program will demand a great deal of sacrifice. Yet, if you love, this fidelity will become sweet and easy to you, for it will help you to grow in love continually.

VII

Three Essential Dispositions

MARY:

My child, the exterior means I have indicated will be useful only insofar as you join to them certain interior dispositions. The same practices lead one soul to sanctity but leave another in mediocrity. "It is the spirit that quickeneth." Listen to what this spirit requires of you.

1. First of all, *self-sacrifice.*

You need it in order to combat your predominant fault relentlessly.

You need it in order to renounce yourself in everything so as not to hinder the action of Jesus in you.

You need it in order to consent to the efforts required for reproducing the dispositions of Jesus.

2. If filial love for me consisted merely in praying

to me, in singing hymns in my honor, and in rejoicing with me, it would hardly require self-sacrifice of you.

But filial love should lead you to identify yourself with Jesus, and this can be accomplished only at the price of complete self-sacrifice.

You cannot serve two masters. The master will be either Jesus or yourself. You must make the choice.

I can help you to renounce yourself; I cannot dispense you from doing so.

3. In the second place, this spirit requires *constancy*.

I can more easily find a hundred souls ready to make a heroic sacrifice in a moment of fervor than one soul capable of persevering every day in the ordinary efforts that fidelity to its resolutions demands.

How often will you not be tempted to abandon such or such a practice which I have suggested to you! Be faithful, cost what it may!

Should you suppress a practice today for some good pretext, tomorrow you will omit it for the first one that comes to mind, and finally you will abandon it entirely without any pretext at all.

Shorten when necessary, but never suppress anything entirely. That is a condition of success.

4. Finally, and above all, you need *generosity*.

There are two sorts of generosity.

The first consists in giving Jesus unhesitatingly not only all He demands but likewise all that pleases Him, even if there is no obligation to do so.

Such was the generosity practiced by your

Mother, and, in varying degrees, by all saintly persons. You must aim at it with all your might.

5. The second kind of generosity consists in regularly making up for your faults and negligences.

If you have committed a fault, offer in compensation a special effort, one which you would not make if you had nothing to expiate. Put into that effort so much love that after your act of reparation you will love Jesus as much as, and even more than you would, if you had not saddened Him.

6. The difference between mediocre and holy souls is not that the former commit faults whereas the latter commit none—for both have their faults—but in this, that the former are content simply to notice their failings, whereas the latter endeavor to love Jesus all the more for having loved Him less in the past. As for yourself, imitate the holy souls in their reparation.

7. In particular make up for any omissions and negligences in your daily conversations with Jesus, in your spiritual renewals, in your daily examinations, and in your retreats.

8. Make your act of reparation follow as quickly as possible upon your fault. A short but immediate act of reparation is worth much more than a prolonged but tardy one.

9. Do you wish to know how to go about these reparations? Consult me after you have fallen or been negligent, and I will teach you how to make of each of your faults a *felix culpa*—a happy fault.

And mind what I say: if you can persevere in being generous as I have just explained, then, despite your sins, defects, temptations, and weakness, I promise to make of you a saint and an apostle.

THE FAITHFUL SOUL:

O Mary, all my activities, all my time, my whole being is yours. Remind me of my consecration to you when I am tempted to be negligent and grant me the generosity of the Saints.

VIII

The Secret of Success

MARY:

My child, the practices and dispositions I have recommended to you will lead you to identify yourself with Jesus only on one condition, namely, that you apply yourself to them under my direction.

1. Jesus has told you: it is the will of the Father who made me Mother of His Son that no one shall perfectly resemble the Son except through me.

2. Sometimes it happens that your ardor cools: spiritual work becomes hard, progress slows down and finally ceases altogether; finally, you begin to lose ground, you retreat! You try to pull yourself together but in vain; then you lose courage. You ask yourself: "What has caused this languidness? What will dispel it?" You do not know.

Well, the first cause of your trouble is invariably a weakening of your union with me, and the first remedy lies in working more faithfully under my direction.

Without me, you cannot succeed; with me, you cannot fail.

3. Do you want success to crown all your efforts? Let me repeat what I have already said, so that you get to realize its importance: Always come to me and submit your plans to me, in order never to act except in my name.

Every time you are about to make a resolution, ask me what I desire of you, and tell me what you decide to do.

4. I am not going to answer you, of course, by a revelation, but, if you come to me in all confidence and with the sincere intention of executing what seems to be my will, you will ordinarily understand whether or not I approve of your resolves. If I seem to approve, confide them to me, so that I may help you realize them. If I do not, pray and reflect; then submit to me another but more precise resolution which I can approve.

5. You will not consult me in this way for very long without perceiving that you advance more rapidly in a few days than you used to in several months, on condition, however, that you really wait for my answer and do not allow your eagerness to carry you ahead too soon. If you faithfully turn to me for a moment before all your actions, I will direct you in everything. Now, there is only one end to which I can direct you: to Jesus, to Jesus who will become the Life of your life.

THE FAITHFUL SOUL:

O Mary, Mother of Good Counsel, enlighten, guide, and assist me now and forever. Amen.

PART 4 — MARY DESCRIBES HER SOLDIER

I

My Mission and Yours

MARY:

My child, listen attentively to what I am going to say and try to understand it well.

1. I have a mystery to reveal to you, a mystery concerning both of us.

2. At the same time that Gabriel announced to me that the Son of God desired to be born of me, he announced that this Son of God, become my Son, would be called *Jesus*, which means Saviour, and I realized that this Saviour wanted to associate me in His work of Redemption. I saw that by consenting to cooperate with the Divine offer, I would be consenting to cooperate not only in the mystery of the Incarnation, but also in that of the Redemption.

I gave my consent.

From that moment until the last sigh of Jesus, I worked with Him in the Redemption of man: I furnished the substance of the Victim and nurtured Him with a view to the final Sacrifice; I united my prayers and sufferings with His; my will with His will; I offered my Son to the Heavenly Father for the supreme Immolation. Jesus was the Redeemer and I was the Co-Redemptrix.

3. Now, understand this well: the calls and the gifts of God are irrevocable. The cooperation which I gave my Son at Nazareth and on Calvary, I must give until the end of time.

Having given Jesus to the entire world on the day of the Incarnation, I must give Him to every human being in particular throughout the ages. Being Co-operatrix with Jesus in the work of the Redemption, I must remain His Co-operatrix in the application of the Redemption to each individual soul. For the Redemption is not yet fully accomplished: the grace of Salvation merited for all on Calvary must still be applied to each man as he comes into this world.

Such is my mission until the end of time. With Jesus I worked at the general Redemption of men; with Jesus I must work at their conversion and sanctification.

4. In fact, could it be otherwise? By becoming the Mother of Jesus, I became the Mother of all those who are destined to be His brothers. Should I not, therefore, like a true mother, watch over the life and the salvation of those to whom I have given birth?

5. As you see, on the day of my entry into Heaven God confided an apostolic mission to me, an apostolic mission that is universal even as was my action as Co-Redemptrix and as is my spiritual Motherhood.

6. I am the Queen of Apostles, not only because I watched over the first Apostles with maternal affection; not only because I obtain fecundity for the work of their successors, who, without my intervention, would be powerless to do the least good to souls; but also because their apostolate is only a limited participation in the universal apostolate first confided to me.

7. This apostolate is a struggle. I must snatch each soul from Satan in order to lead it to Jesus and to the Father.

At the moment of the Tempter's triumph over our first parents, God foretold him his defeat: "I will put enmities between thee and the woman, and thy posterity and her posterity: she shall crush thy head."

I crushed his head already at the first moment of my Immaculate Conception. But that victory was only the first of an infinite series of victories. Even to the end of time I must crush his head. I am his irreconcilable adversary, "more terrible than an army in battle array."

8. In the struggle for souls, I already defeated him while the Church was in its infancy. Since then I have destroyed every heresy in the entire world and have brought innumerable sinners back to the path of salvation.

Now, God has decreed that from century to century, my conquering action should become more and more manifest. In these later times, He wishes it to appear before the eyes of all with unprecedented clearness.

9. Satan seems to be triumphing in the world

today. But fear not; precisely because his power is growing, God wishes me to appear more openly in order to crush his head. A tremendous victory is reserved for me. My kingdom must be established throughout the world so that the Kingdom of my Son may come more fully.

Have you not noticed that Jesus is much better known, loved, and served since the proclamation of my Immaculate Conception? that His Person, His Eucharist, His Sacred Heart, His Kingship are more ardently and loyally honored than they were for centuries? "Of His kingdom there shall be no end," said the Archangel Gabriel to me. But now, as then, it is I who must give the world its King.

The last age of the Church shall be, more than any other, my age. You shall see marvels operated by and for me. You shall see Satan crushed to the earth by the heel of a woman—crushed as he never was before. You shall see the Church displaying a fecundity and a conquering power above all that she has ever known. You shall see Jesus reigning over ever-increasing multitudes and acclaimed by the very ones who opposed Him most bitterly.

10. Such is my part in the mystery which I wished to reveal to you.

And now here is your part:

God decided to associate men, and especially certain men, in the execution of His works of love, and to make the success of these works depend upon the fidelity of these men to their vocation.

In order to continue on earth the mission which He had received from His Father, Jesus willed to rely upon the assistance of the Apostles and their successors. In the same way, in order to carry out my mission of conquest in the world, I need auxiliaries and soldiers.

When will men see the marvels which I have foretold? Only when my children understand my apostolic role and consent to battle under my orders and at my side.

11. You have understood this role. Do you wish to be my soldier? Do you wish to aid me in rescuing my children from Satan and leading them to Jesus? Do you wish to share in the victory reserved for me?

Following the example of your divine Model, you have given yourself entirely to me. You have consecrated to me your body and soul, your thoughts, words, and deeds. Now that you understand how I wish to use your person and your powers, are you going to retract your consecration?

12. In the idea of filial love for me, you at first saw only the attitude of the child on His Mother's lap. And here I am, leading you onto a battlefield. Still, was Jesus my Child only in the sheltered home of Nazareth? Was He not just as truly mine while He was destroying the empire of the prince of this world and redeeming the human race? Did He not become my Son precisely because He wished to be the Saviour of men?

He has likewise called you to be my child of predilection, so that you, too, may become a saviour of souls. You must either become an apostle therefore, or renounce the honor of being my child of predilection.

73

THE FAITHFUL SOUL:

O Mary, I am entirely yours, and everything I possess belongs to you.

For you and under your orders I wish to work, fight, suffer, and die. My battle cry will be *"Maria duce*! Under Mary's leadership!"

II

The Flame of Zeal

MARY:

You are resolved to be my apostle, but you wonder how in your present situation you can be one. If you are not invested with the priesthood, you have received no mission to preach.

1. Look about you, my son. Do you see those propagators of revolutionary doctrines who periodically succeed one another in the world and who win over millions of followers in a few years? With what priesthood are they clothed? Who gave them the mission to preach? Many of them have had to brave insults, persecutions, imprisonments, sometimes even the scaffold or the firing squad, in order to attain their purpose; but they had become passionate apostles of an idea, or rather of a diabolic lie—and they succeeded.

And you, the apostle of Christ and of His Mother, you wonder how you can succeed.

2. Do not argue that these apostles of falsehood have it easy, since they have but to flatter the

passions, and men will applaud. You have means of success that are much more powerful. To satisfy the profound aspirations of men, you have the doctrine of the Truth which makes them free, the secret of happiness which satisfies them, the knowledge of the Unknown God whom they long for, and as support you have the all-powerful assistance of God.

3. Did the first preachers of the Gospel flatter the passions of the pagans and the Jews? Did they not rather preach painful sacrifices and the obligation of being ready to suffer persecution, imprisonment, fire, and the sword? Yet they converted countless multitudes with amazing rapidity, and all because there burned in them the sacred flame of apostolic zeal!

Ah! had that flame burned as intensely in the hearts of their successors, the name of my Son would have been preached to every creature centuries ago.

4. It is this flame that you must kindle in your soul! How? Come, follow me to Calvary. Place yourself next to me and look at Jesus Crucified. See His Body trembling under those frightful tortures. Above all, see His soul a prey to agony a thousandfold more frightful. What is it that fills Him with that infinite desolation? It is, to a great extent, the vision of countless men for whom He is shedding His Blood in vain. In vain, doubtless, because they will resist the call of grace; but in vain also, because those who should continue the saving work of the Redemption in their behalf will neglect their charge.

5. Listen! Jesus is speaking: "Woman, behold thy son; behold thy Mother." It is to me and to you that He speaks.

O my son, sound the depths of my sorrows. Why did I have to undergo this martyrdom? Because of the torments that racked the Body of Jesus, but especially because of the agony of His soul. For, together with Him I was contemplating the multitudes of men to whom I was giving birth and who, I foresaw, would simply rush on to eternal perdition.

6. "Woman, behold thy son! He will aid you to save your children—children who without his help would be eternally lost. He will lead those poor erring creatures back to you. He will help you in your apostolic mission and bring consolation to us both."

Have you grasped the desires of Jesus?

Oh! may the spectacle of Calvary haunt you, pursue you relentlessly! May the cry of the dying Christ and the sighs of your suffering Mother resound night and day in your ears! Then you will really get to be an apostle.

7. Listen again! "I thirst! I thirst in My Body; I thirst above all in My Heart. Will he who replaces Me at My Mother's side, give Me the souls I crave?"

THE FAITHFUL SOUL:

O my Mother, never allow me to forget my three loves: Jesus, Mary, and souls!

III

Apostolic Prayer

MARY:

My child, do you realize that in whatever circumstances you may be you have at your disposal a most efficacious weapon for apostolic action: prayer?

1. You believe doubtless that the salvation of souls can be advanced by prayer as well as by preaching. You admit that prayer is a consoling substitute for action in the case of old folks, the sick and all those who cannot engage in exterior works of zeal.

But how far you are from understanding the power that prayer has in the apostolate!

2. Prayer is not a substitute for direct action: it is an apostolic weapon whose effectiveness far surpasses that of any exterior activity.

Jesus preached during three years, but He first prayed for thirty years. During those three years of exterior apostolate He not only passed whole nights in prayer, but while His lips were busy instructing the children of men, He also constantly communed with His Heavenly Father in His innermost soul.

I cooperated with Him in the work of Redemption. I never preached; I never directed the Church; I never worked miracles; but I did pray and I did suffer.

And Joseph, like myself, prayed and suffered. Without uttering so much as one word which has been recorded in a book, he accomplished more for the conversion of mankind than did St. John, St. Paul, and St. Peter.

Examine the lives of men devoted to the apostolate: all those who had extraordinary success in converting souls, were also extraordinarily given to prayer.

3. Woe to the apostle who does not pray! He is but sounding brass and a tinkling cymbal; he spends himself and wearies himself and perhaps loses his own soul without doing any good to the souls of others. If his activity seems nevertheless to produce fruits of salvation, these fruits are due to the earnest prayers of some soul unknown to him and unaware of the good it is accomplishing, and therefore he himself will receive no reward for it.

4. Could it be otherwise? To convert, sanctify, and save a soul is a supernatural work. Can anything supernatural be accomplished by merely natural means?

Supernatural achievements are the fruit of grace and grace is the fruit of prayer. The more you pray, the more supernatural work you will achieve.

5. God wants exterior works wherever they are possible, just as He wants the sensible sign in order to produce sacramental grace. But just as a whole ocean of water is, of itself, powerless to cleanse the soul of a babe, so all exterior actions are powerless to convert or to sanctify a single man.

The word of the priest must accompany the pouring of the water upon the infant's brow; the prayer of the apostle must accompany his exterior action.

Prayer can even completely replace action wherever action is impossible, just as Baptism of desire may replace Baptism by water when the latter is impossible.

6. Is not God almighty? Has He not infinite means of sending the grace of salvation to souls? He can endow a single word with marvelous effectiveness. He can arrange that a word which is heard or read and perhaps misunderstood in a moment of sudden misfortune or in some commonplace occurrence will be the lesson needed to enlighten and touch the heart and turn it to God. He can even make use of His enemies to have His merciful plans realized. The prophet Balaam was sent to curse Israel, but he ended by pronouncing a blessing instead.

What is lacking in our apostolate is not so much external deeds as apostolic prayer.

7. Have you grasped this lesson, my child?

If so, do you endeavor to be an apostle more by prayer than by exterior action? Do you think of praying every day with an apostolic aim in view?

When you wish to win a soul, you think over the steps to be taken and the things to be said—and you do well. But do you apply yourself to prayer with even greater earnestness? Do you base your hope of success on God to whom you pray, rather than on your own skill and persuasive power?

8. Pray! Pray! and learn to pray more and more for the conversion and sanctification of souls!

To each of your daily prayers and Communions, add an apostolic intention.

Transform your actions and sufferings into prayers by offering them to God through my hands for some special purpose according to my intentions.

Offer up too, all the Masses said and all the Rosaries prayed throughout the world during the day.

Apply to monasteries and convents of contemplatives and to all the humble confident souls that can help you by their supplications, and ask for prayers. Above all, get the cooperation of the sick and of souls that suffer: their prayers and sacrifices have an almost Sacramental power.

9. Pray for your parents and for all those who are dear to you.

Pray for the Church, for the Pope, for the bishops and priests, and for all missionaries and apostles.

Pray in particular for those who like yourself have assembled under my banner to hasten the advent of the Kingdom of Jesus by hastening the advent of mine.

Pray for those to whom you have sought to do good, that that good may remain.

Pray for those to whom you should have done good, that your prayer may repair your negligence.

Pray for those whom you will meet in the course of the day, so that you may do them all the good which God wants you to do them.

10. Pray before taking action, so that God grants it the success which He desires. Pray when action looms up difficult before you, so that your prayer compensates for your weakness. Pray when all

seems easy, lest, relying on your natural skill, you should produce no supernatural results.

Pray during your activities, so that God continues to act through you.

Pray after your actions to thank God if you have succeeded, or to beg Him to accomplish His work nevertheless if you seem to have failed, knowing that the more God compels you to pray, the more success He wishes to give you.

Pray, and never stop praying! Then you will accomplish marvels through me and for me.

THE FAITHFUL SOUL:

O you, whose life was a ceaseless prayer for the glory of the Father, the mission of the Son, and the salvation of your children, teach me how to pray.

IV

The Redeeming Cross

MARY:

My child, listen and try to understand. I wish to teach you a doctrine which is all the more difficult to grasp because you imagine you are quite familiar with it: the doctrine of Salvation by the Cross.

1. All those who take part in the Christian apostolate know that suffering plays a paramount role in the saving of souls; they know that Jesus delivered the world from the bondage of sin by

His Passion and death, that I had to become the Mother of Sorrows in order to become the Co-Redemptrix, and that all great apostles passed through great tribulations.

But when it is upon them that suffering comes, they forget its significance. They are surprised and discouraged. For them, as for the Jews, the Cross remains a stumbling block. Do they imagine that they can take part in Christ's redeeming action unless they also share in His redeeming Passion?

2. As for yourself, look courageously at the cross which awaits you.

You will have to make difficult sacrifices. You will have to labor and to suffer, to spend and exhaust yourself in the service of souls—and that, not only during a few hours or days, but just as long as there will be souls to save; not only in moments of enthusiasm and success, but also in moments of difficulty and disgust.

3. To these trials, which are the price that must be paid for any apostolate, even a natural one, you will have to add voluntary sacrifices. To the hard labors of the three years of His public ministry Jesus chose to add the sufferings of His Passion and death. He longed for this Baptism of Blood; He offered Himself because He wanted to do so.

Like Him you will have to make yourself a victim in behalf of the souls that you wish to redeem.

Before every apostolic effort, in addition to praying, offer some sacrifice.

If the work is particularly difficult, prepare and accompany it with particularly hard sacrifices.

If you have not succeeded after the use of ordinary means, do not say: "I have worked, preached, pleaded, and prayed; I have done all I could." So long as you have not really sacrificed yourself, you have no right to say that. And if you repeat it to yourself to console yourself in failure, you are a weakling and a hypocrite.

4. To an apostle who makes generous sacrifices, God sends all sorts of trials as a special reward: sickness, poverty, disappointments, dryness, darkness, the impression he is nothing but a hindrance, failures due to his character, ignorance, or imprudence. These crosses, if accepted with faith, humility, and love, purify him of all self-seeking, show his absolute personal incapacity, make him cast himself into the arms of God as his last hope, and thus render his efforts incomparably more fruitful than do the mortifications of his own choosing.

5. Are you ready to embrace these crosses? Perhaps you are.

But there is another cross much more difficult to carry because it is so disconcerting.

Your intentions will be misunderstood, your plans ridiculed, your activity blamed. Those to whom you might look for aid will prove indifferent to your work or else will go about tearing down what you have tried to build up. Those who should encourage you will disown you and put a stop to your enterprises. All kinds of obstacles will be raised against you, and people will declare with satisfaction: "I always said he would fail!"

The cross of your own choosing you carry joyfully enough. The cross imposed upon you by sickness or poverty you succeed in accepting with resignation. But the cross prepared for you by the ignorance, the stupidity, or the malice of men threatens to disgust you.

Still, it is just this last cross which has the greatest redemptive power.

6. Look at Jesus. Was it self-imposed suffering with which He saved you? Was it not rather the suffering caused by the ignorance, the stupidity, and the maliciousness of men—of the very men whose functions and profession should have prompted them to aid Him in the work of redeeming their nation.

7. Do not be astonished if the devil tries to ruin your work. When he attacks my soldiers, he is really attacking me. Keep up your confidence and courage. As a result his defeat will be all the more complete: I have crushed his head, and I will continue to crush it forever.

8. But remember that suffering has no redemptive power of itself, but only when united with the sufferings of Jesus.

The same law holds for your suffering as for your person. Alone, you are only a weak sinner; united to Jesus, you participate in His Divine nature. So also, suffering by itself remains unfruitful, but once it is united to the sufferings of Jesus, it participates in their Divine efficacy.

9. When sorrow comes to you in your apostolic labors, come and press closer to me. Together we shall climb up to Calvary. There, close to the Cross of the Redeemer, you will understand the infinite

value of that suffering which puzzled and crushed you previously.

In the shadow of the Cross, even the suffering caused by the stupid and malicious men will become sweet to you. In it you will consider not the men who cause it, but Jesus and your Mother who thus invite you to participate in their redeeming mission; in it you will consider the souls which this redeeming mission will enable you to save.

10. This is a severe doctrine that I am preaching to you, my child, but it is a doctrine of Faith, of love, and of victory.

Did I go too far when I presumed you were able to understand it?

THE FAITHFUL SOUL:

O Mother, you know my cowardice and fear of suffering; but you also know my desire to love you and to assist you in your mission.

When trials overwhelm me, you will be my support, and then I shall be capable of suffering all that you desire, because you desire it, cost what it may!

V

Preaching by Your Life

MARY:

My child, the indirect apostolate of prayer and suffering is marvelously fruitful, but you must join to it the direct action of soul upon soul.

1. You think I mean the apostolate of the Word. That is important, no doubt, but there is another which should precede, accompany, and follow it: the apostolate of a good life.

2. You do not need much experience in life to realize that certain souls remain untouched by even the most eloquent words.

Words are fruitful only if received in a soul disposed to receive them. If they fall on stony ground or among thorns, how can they bear fruit? It is the example of a good life that will dispose souls to listen to your words.

An action, a gesture, a look, or a smile often does more good than a long sermon.

3. Make people esteem your Religion for what they see in you.

Always be respectable and remember your greatness as a Christian in whom you know God Himself has made His dwelling. Let people near you feel something of that mysterious Presence which they experience near the Tabernacle.

Let your virtue be above suspicion in the midst of universal corruption.

Be honest and upright, although persons about you think only of enriching themselves at their neighbor's expense.

Be straightforward and sincere even though lying and dissimulation have become the rule almost everywhere.

Be conscientious and faithful in your duties even in the midst of persons who seem to have lost the very notions of duty and conscience.

May those who do not share your Faith, and

even those who attack it, find themselves obliged to esteem it by the very fact that they esteem the conduct to which it inspires you.

4. Strive to appear just what you are, without display and yet without human respect.

What have you to blush about? About possessing the Truth when others know nothing but error? About retaining your dignity as a human being while they submit to the bondage of degrading passion? About being the disciple of Christ and the soldier of His Mother?

Are you afraid of not being esteemed by those who think or act differently from you? Have you never noticed that men, even the most perverse, esteem those who dare to have personal convictions and to live up to them?

Be a Christian who knows no fear and gives no ground for reproach; and your conduct will be a constant sermon.

5. It is a grand achievement to make the doctrine of Christ esteemed in your own person. But go still further: make men *love* it.

Take an interest in others; do them all the favors you can; listen to their complaints; relieve them in misfortune; dress their wounds; assist them in their toil; be obliging and kind to all those who come to you; make yourself all things to all men and you will gain all men to Christ.

If they feel happier because of you, they will end by loving those ideas which made you a source of happiness.

By contact with you let them grasp better the meaning of affection, and they will better understand what God is, even if they do not know Him by name—for God is not a name, God is Love. By opening their hearts to love, they open them to God.

6. In order to make yourself all things to all men, you must not consider their qualities or defects, their virtues or vices, their actions, good or bad; you must see in them the price of the Sacred Blood of Jesus and of my immense sorrow. Love them with the same love with which their Redeemer and their Mother love them, and you will win them over to love, and through love, to God.

THE FAITHFUL SOUL:

Mother, I have seen a number of your children, whose lives were a continual exhortation, whereas I so often shock the persons near me. With you I too will make an effort to preach Jesus henceforth by my conduct. Grant that, when people see me, they will feel drawn nearer to Him.

VI

The Saving Word

MARY:

My child, learn to speak as an apostle, in order to spread the spirit of Christ about you.

1. Do not say, "I have no opportunity of doing so." The opportunity exists, look for it: if none exists, create one.

Child of light as you are, must I send you to the children of darkness to learn a few lessons? They know how to find opportunities all about them for disseminating their false doctrines: in the intimacy of a conversation, in the street, in the workshop, in the train, and even in their amusements. Can you not do for the salvation of souls what they do for the ruin of them?

And do not forget: If you think you are powerless to do good, what you lack is not the opportunity for good, but the fire of apostolic zeal. Come and renew it on Calvary, and you will find abundant opportunities to spread it far and wide.

2. To speak as an apostle, you need not preach.

On all occasions, let your religious convictions inspire your words. Whether your talk be of persons, things, or events, let your thoughts be those of Christ, and dare to express them.

Seldom dispute with adversaries; never humiliate them. Simply explain your ideas.

Truth by its very nature is attractive, for it is the Truth which sets men free. Of itself it is made to conquer, because its splendor invites assent.

Do not imagine that you must ordinarily make long discourses. A short explanation, a discreet counsel, a simple reflection, sometimes a mere interjection may suffice to make a sincere soul find the light.

3. Remember, the thing which convinces people is not so much what you say as what you are.

Speak simply but courageously: the infallible Truth is yours.

Let people feel that you are deeply convinced

of what you say. If your life always conforms to your teaching, they will readily believe you.

Let them see that you are more interested in doing good to others than in winning a victory.

Study the doctrine of Christ incessantly so that you will live it better and bear more witness to it by your life.

Become an expert in your profession. If you are competant in your trade or profession, you will be considered an authority in your teaching of religious doctrine.

4. It is only after a long apprenticeship that you will become skillful in the apostolate of souls.

Before each conversation, ask me to dictate what you should say.

After talking, examine in my presence whether you have been successful in making someone better and happier, and see how you can be more successful next time.

The more you allow yourself to be directed by me in this apprenticeship, the more rapid and perfect will be your progress. It is for me and through me that you should become an apostle.

THE FAITHFUL SOUL:

Mary, I admit that I have rarely tried to propagate your Son's doctrine, because in my social contacts I was preoccupied only about myself. Henceforth I will think of Jesus and souls. I will pray to you before speaking and you will let me know what I am to say.

In Union There Is Strength

MARY:

My child, do not remain isolated.

1. Join with others who have the same apostolic aspirations as yourself.

Keeping the sacred fire of the apostolate buried in the depths of your soul will smother it.

By speaking with others about ideas and ideals which are common to you, you will increase your enthusiasm as well as theirs.

Union with others will do more than inflame the zeal of all of you; it will make it uncommonly strong.

If you work with another, you will be not twice but ten times as strong. And if you form a closely united battalion marching under my banner, you will be invincible.

2. Where will you find those fellow soldiers animated with the same ambitions as yourself?

Seek and you shall find.

Perhaps there are some right next to you, all ready to welcome you into their ranks. Join them.

If you can enroll in one of my sodalities, no matter what it is called, do not hesitate to do so. In the past, those sodalities whose members realized that they constituted not merely a devotional association but a militia advancing in the name of the Woman predestined to crush the head of the Serpent, have won brilliant victories. In the future, victories yet more brilliant will be granted them, according as they understand better and better my mission and theirs.

Or, if circumstances lead you to it, join the Legion of Mary. In the course of its triumphant progress all over the world, it has worked miracles of conversion and spiritual transformation. That is not surprising, however, to those who know that where Mary Immaculate passes, miracles seem to spring up in her footsteps.

Perhaps about you there are only isolated individuals. Make it your business to discover among them those who are capable of understanding your views.

It often happens that in a given locality several persons have identical interests and ambitions, yet each one, ignorant of the other, believes he is alone. And when, after months or perhaps years, a chance conversation happens to reveal one to the other, they are quite astonished to find that they took each other for strangers so long, whereas they were really brothers.

Try to speak to others of what you hold dear, and you will discover what response your advances arouse.

3. At first, you will perhaps not find those who can share your ideal. Nor will your best collaborators always be those who respond first and most enthusiastically to your advances. A sound judgment, a steady will, generosity, and a capacity for devotedness are worth much more than sudden bursts of fervor.

Do not object: "Nothing can be done here. The people round about me are all indifferent." There are noble hearts which hide; there are generous souls quite unaware of their own generosity. It is for you to make them realize what they are capable of. They will be supremely happy to feel longings for perfection and a devotion to a great cause awaken within them.

4. At times the very men who profess doctrines diametrically opposed to yours will be the most apt to become some day your comrades. Did not Saul, the great persecutor, become Paul, the great Apostle of Christ? Judge the character of a man less by his words and actions than by the interior dispositions underlying them. A sincere, ardent, generous unbeliever is better fitted to fight your spiritual battles with you than is a Christian who lacks energy and the spirit of sacrifice.

5. You may perhaps have to search a long time, exhaust your strength forming co-workers, and endure many a cruel deception. Be not disheartened. Christ has His chosen ones in every class of society; seek and you shall find.

6. In the beginning you will be perhaps only a small company. It matters not, provided you are closely united. Majorities do not triumph in this world, but the active, resolute, well-organized and well-disciplined minorities do.

With an infallible and marvelously effective doctrine, with unrivaled virtue and devotedness, with the sublimest ideals, and with the all-powerful assistance of Heaven, Catholics of almost every land have more than they need for the triumph of their cause, if only they knew how to unite. But they do not know, and hence in nearly every land it is they who are vanquished.

The enemies of my Son are divided on all points of doctrine; they unite only to attack the Church. Catholics are united on all points of doctrine; they are divided only when they defend the Church.

If Satan finds Christians too zealous in the service of God to be likely to succumb to temptations against faith or purity, he inspires them with opposing apostolic methods and then instead of fighting him they fight one another.

Have they never observed that in war the victorious nation is the one whose soldiers and officers forget personal views and cooperate faithfully in some general plan of campaign, even though it may not be the best? Have they never observed that in the conquests of the Church, the troops which have ever enjoyed the greatest success are the companies of religious obliged by their vow of obedience to follow with perfect docility the direction of their leaders?

7. Who are the leaders who will coordinate your action with that of your fellow soldiers?

God "hath placed the bishops to rule His Church." The Bishop of Bishops has given clear orders to his armies: You must serve me within the framework of Catholic Action wherever it is possible to do so. Have you already studied the purposes and program of this wonderful institution? Do you know how it is organized in your diocese? Have you tried to find out how you could most effectively take a hand in it?

8. No matter what your personal preferences may be, try to understand that a small result

which is really achieved is worth more than a greater one that is not achieved; that there is no strength without union, and no union without self-sacrifice; and that the triumph of the common cause is to be preferred to the triumph of one's personal ideas.

Think over these principles, live them, and teach them to others!

THE FAITHFUL SOUL:

Mother, I intend to work all my life, I assure you, at increasing your forces and at making them more united, strong, and enthusiastic.

VIII

"Those Who Teach Me. . ."

MARY:

My child, Jesus has brought you to me so that, once you have become my child of predilection, you may also become my apostle. Everything you undertake under my direction, He will bless. Yet He wishes you not only to act in my name but also to preach my name to others, and every time you do so He will attach a special grace and power to your apostolate.

1. Being an apostle means bringing souls to Christ and giving Christ to souls. I am the way which leads to Christ; it is I who gave Christ to the world. Do you want to lead souls more rapidly to Christ? Then show them the way which leads

to Him. Do you wish to give Him to them fully? Show them her whose mission it is to give Him to souls.

Recall your own experience. Despite your constant infidelity to grace, have you not remarked an astonishing transformation in yourself ever since Jesus revealed the mystery of His filial love to you? You have found the light, do not hide it under a bushel, but rather make it shine before men. The secret of your improved interior life will also be the secret of a more efficient apostolic life. The more manifestly you introduce me into your exterior action, the more successful you will make it.

2. It is Jesus who has so willed it. He could have given Himself directly to men, but He decided to give Himself only through me. In the prophecy made in the Garden of Eden and in the declarations of the Prophets, as well as in His manifestations to the shepherds and the Magi, to St. Simeon and St. Anne, at Cana and on Calvary, He willed to make me known to men at the same time as He made Himself known to them.

Through His Church, His Mystical Body animated with His Spirit, He never stops preaching me and teaching that the most natural way to find Him is to go to the Son by way of the Mother.

He has taught you to imitate His filial love towards me. Imitate this particular aspect of His filial love.

3. I have explained to you how, especially in these latter days, Jesus wishes to glorify my name and to have me more known and honored, in order

thereby to sanctify and save souls. In this great victory which He has reserved for me they especially will share who manifest me to men.

Make me known as much as you can. Jesus expects it of you.

4. I, too, expect it of you.

I have so many children who do not know their Mother or who know her very little. It is for you to reveal her to them, so that she can embrace them also, as her beloved children. It is for you to lead them to her, that she may form them as she does you to the likeness of her Firstborn Son.

5. How can you make me known and loved?

There is one way which is infallible. Fill yourself with a burning love for me and for souls and you will know how to preach about me.

First, let people know that you are particularly devoted to my service. Do not be afraid to let them see you with my rosary or my medal, or at some public festival in my honor. If at the same time you show yourself a fearless, irreproachable Christian, your conduct will be a most eloquent sermon in my honor.

6. Then, at the propitious moment, drop a word here and there which will reveal your convictions and your experience regarding your life of union with me.

In intimate conversation or correspondence can you not sometimes mention my name?

To a heart oppressed with grief can you not recall the thought of the Comforter of the Afflicted?

To souls who are struggling to preserve or recover their virtue, can you not recommend recourse to the

Immaculate Virgin, who has received from her Son the mission of making all those pure who invoke her?

To souls who yearn for intimacy with Jesus can you not let fall some hint as to how you became more closely united to Him?

To souls eager for apostolic work can you not explain the mission of conquest which God has confided to me and the wonderful fruitfulness which will assuredly accompany their efforts if they fight in my name and under my orders?

And if you ever have the opportunity to make me known by speaking in public or by writing, hasten to profit by that call of grace. Your words will bear a message of confidence, love and salvation to all those willing souls whom they reach and through them, perhaps, to thousands more.

"Those who make me known to others shall have life everlasting," and shall procure it for many others round about them.

THE FAITHFUL SOUL:

"Make me worthy of praising you, O Blessed Virgin.

"Give me strength against your enemies."

IX

At Thy Word I Will Let Down the Net

MARY:

You are beginning to understand by what means you may carry on your apostolate, but you are far from understanding with what confidence you should go about it.

1. Sometimes, as you think over how weak you are and how difficult the task confided to you is, you start to ask yourself, "What can I really do?"

What can you do? By yourself, nothing. With me, wonderful things.

Was it not because He who is mighty looked upon the nothingness of His handmaid that He accomplished great things in her? Have you never read that "the foolish things of the world hath God chosen, that He may confound the wise; and the weak things of the world hath God chosen, that He may confound the strong"?

2. Listen to my words and meditate upon them. I want you to understand two truths which will give you an invincible faith in the success of your mission, a faith which will move mountains.

To begin with, remember that your apostolate is my apostolate, and that your interests are mine.

It was to me, not to you, that God confided the mission of crushing the Serpent's head and of establishing the Kingdom of my Son in this world; you only participate in my mission. I am the commandress-in-chief of the army of Christ; you are merely my soldier. It is my children, not yours, who must be saved. Does not a mother desire the salvation of her children much more ardently than a stranger would? Does not the general wish for victory much more intensely than the mere private does? Are not the interests of Jesus infinitely more precious to me than to you?

Even if you were indifferent to your success,

surely I could not remain indifferent, for it is my Son, Jesus, and all my other children who are at stake.

Now, I am all-powerful through the omnipotence of God, and I can confer this omnipotence on those who act in my name.

3. Secondly, call to mind and apply to your apostolate the words of Jesus about the unlimited confidence you should have in prayers:

a) I have a loving intention regarding each of your apostolic enterprises.

b) This intention always surpasses in perfection any which you could imagine. For, I love you more than you love yourself, and I love Jesus and souls more than you could ever love them.

c) This intention is always perfectly realizable.

d) It will be realized infallibly in proportion as you act in my name.

Hence, whatever the obstacles, you can always succeed beyond your expectations provided you act in my name.

4.) Yet, in order to win these marvelous victories, it is not enough that you work hard; you must work *in my name*.

The Apostles had wearied themselves fishing all night, and had caught nothing. Yet scarcely had St. Peter said to Jesus, "At Thy word, I will let down the net," when they made a miraculous draught of fishes.

How often have you not spent yourself in apostolic work, but all in vain! The reason was that you started without saying to me: "In thy name..."

Working in my name means working according to my intentions and with a consciousness that you are sharing in my mission and in my omnipotence.

5. Offer your prayers and suffering to Jesus through my hands so that my intentions for your apostolate may be realized.

Before starting anything, pray to me and see what my intentions may be, so that you may act as my instrument.

Begin with supreme confidence in your success, because it is I who am working through you.

Be careful not to let your ideas take the place of mine.

How often you begin by protesting that you are acting only for me, but soon you allow yourself to be directed by your own interests!

You will be certain of success only if you persevere in the disposition of acting according to my intentions. Peter, in the midst of the storm, started across the water with a firm faith in Jesus, who had commanded him to come. Then he thought of the waves and of himself, and began to sink. Often you have begun to accomplish wonderful things only to have them end in failure. The reason was that you had lost the sense of being my instrument.

6. You cannot indeed, be thinking of me at every moment, yet you can remain constantly under the influence of my spirit. You can attain to such a disposition that if someone would ask you, "In whose name are you working?" you could answer: "In the name of my Mother."

You will not acquire such a disposition until you have made many an effort. At least renew your intentions from time to time, and rectify them whenever you find that you have substituted your own views for mine.

7. If after the work is done, you feel you have succeeded, thank God.

If you seem to have failed, examine yourself: either you have not acted in my name and your failure is real; or you have tried to conform to my intentions and to rely on me, and success is merely delayed. It will come in God's good time and will be all the more glorious, because it will have cost greater effort and demanded more confidence. Thus Our Lord will be glorified, your Mother honored, and souls rescued from damnation.

Without me, you cannot succeed. With me, you cannot fail.

THE FAITHFUL SOUL:

O my Mother, I believe in you and in the mission which Jesus has confided to you. I believe that in leaning upon you I shall be all-powerful.

Make me fail quite noticeably each time that I act for myself, in order to compel me to act only for you.

Then shall I effectively help you lead many souls to Jesus, and the prayer which I love to repeat every hour of the day and every time that I awake during the night will come true: "May the Father, the Son and the Holy Ghost be glorified in all places through the Immaculate Virgin Mary."

Jesus Sums Up the Ideal

JESUS:

My brother, do you understand the gift which I made in revealing to you the mystery of My filial love for My Mother? When I called you to give yourself entirely to her as I did, you saw in My appeal only an invitation to love her a trifle more than you loved her before. Now, little by little, you have learned that to imitate My filial love for her is to become under her guidance a saint and an apostle, to be transformed into Me, the Son of God become Son of Mary for the salvation of the world.

THE FAITHFUL SOUL:

Jesus, my God and my Brother!
Mary, Mother of God and my Mother!
Once more, I give myself to you unreservedly and forever, but with a clearer understanding of your plans for me and with a stronger determination to carry them out at any cost.

O Jesus, grant me the grace to love Your Mother and to make her loved everywhere with the same love with which You loved her.

And you, O Mary, obtain for me the grace to love Jesus and to make Him loved by all men as you yourself love Him.

CONSECRATION TO MARY

Entire consecration to Mary constitutes an essential element of filial and apostolic devotion to Mary considered as a participation in the filial love of Jesus towards His Mother as taught in this book. It is therefore important to make this consecration a memorable event in one's existence and the starting point of a new life.

It is good to choose a feast of the Blessed Virgin or of Our Lord for pronouncing this consecration, and to make a month of special preparation for it. Every day of this month it would be well to say the Rosary or at least one decade of the Rosary and to read reflectively a chapter of *My Ideal*. (This little book comprises thirty-one chapters, but chapters II and III of Part 2 may be read together as one.)

On the feast chosen for it, either after Holy Communion or at some other more suitable moment of the day, the Act of Consecration given below should be read slowly.

This sort of consecration is supposed to be permanent. To assure this perpetuity not only by a promise made perhaps in a moment of fervor but also by a really irrevocable decision of the will, some servants of Mary oblige themselves to it by vow. Father Chaminade, whose teachings are reproduced in this book, gave his disciples who form the Society of Mary a special vow of stability or of perseverance in the service of Mary which has been recognized by the Holy See as a fourth religious vow. Persons who do not belong to the Society of Mary can follow the example of certain servants of Mary and prohibit themselves by vow from ever retracting their consecration to Mary.

They may even bind themselves under pain of sin to some special obligation and, for example, consecrate their body to Mary by a vow of chastity, or their possessions by renouncing all use of them contrary to what they believe are Mary's intentions, or their will by binding themselves always to do what they are sure is Mary's will, which is of course always the same as God's will.

Some go as far as to bind themselves never to refuse the Blessed Virgin what she clearly desires of them.

Before obliging one's self to some practice by vow, it is good to bind one's self for some time by simple promise. Before making any vow, one should consult one's confessor or spiritual director.

For making the consecration, the following formula may be used:

ACT OF CONSECRATION TO MARY

O Mary, Virgin Immaculate, I firmly believe that the Son of God chose you to be His true Mother.

I believe that, being your Son, He loved you and continues to love you more than all other creatures, and that He performed all the duties of a loving Son with infinite perfection.

I believe that He has deigned to associate you in His mission of Redemption; that, in accordance with His will, no soul, guilty or innocent, will be sanctified and saved without your mediation; and that no one will come to Him except through you.

I believe that, being His Mother, you are also mine. For, when you conceived Him at Nazareth, you conceived me; when you sacrificed Him on Calvary, you brought me forth to supernatural life; when you cooperate with Him in the distribution of all graces, you continue to nourish me and to educate me as another Jesus.

I believe that He desires me to imitate His example and to strive as much as possible to be to you what He Himself always was and always will be.

Behold, I give and consecrate myself to you as your child, just as Jesus gave Himself to be your Son.

I give you my body and my soul, whatever I have, am, do, and can do.

I give myself unreservedly and irrevocably, for time and for eternity.

I give myself so that you may use me as you wish, demand of me any act of devotedness, impose upon me any sacrifice—those that I foresee and those that are hidden from me, those that will be sweet and those at which nature will rebel.

I fear nothing, I know to whom I am giving myself.

After the example of Jesus, I wish to love you with all the powers of my soul; I wish to honor, to obey, to imitate you; I wish to have full confidence in you, to be united constantly with you, and in short to reproduce with the utmost perfection all the dispositions of the filial love of your Divine Son, and to become, under your tutelage, another Jesus in your regard.

I particularly wish to assist you in your providential mission. I wish to be your apostle and soldier in the warfare against Satan. I wish to combat in your name and to save your children from his grasp. I wish to fight for the glory of your name, to make you known, loved, and served. I am convinced that revealing you to men is the most effective way of revealing Jesus to them.

I am only a poor sinner—you know it well— full of defects, weaker and more inconstant than I can realize. But I put my confidence in you. I am not working in my own name. I shall be omnipotent because you are omnipotent with the Divine power of your Son, and because my interests are your interests and my cause is your cause. I shall battle under your orders, confident that you will win the victory.

O Mary, Mother of Jesus, and my Mother, for the glory of the Most Holy Trinity, for your honor, and for the salvation of my soul and the souls of others, accept the offering I am making of myself to you and obtain for me the grace to be faithful to it to the end of my days. Amen.

(Only if applicable: O Jesus, in order to make this complete consecration of myself to Your Mother as sacred and irrevocable as possible, I hereby bind myself by vow never to retract it, and to observe the following particular practice: ...Give me the grace to live up to my consecration all the days of my life and unto my last breath.)

SHORT ACT OF CONSECRATION

O Mary, Mother of Jesus and my Mother, I give myself entirely to you, in order to imitate as perfectly as possible the filial love of Jesus for you and to battle under your orders for the conquest of souls. Amen.

COLLECTIVE ACT OF CONSECRATION

Sovereign Mistress of Heaven and earth, at the foot of thy throne, where respect and love have enchained our hearts, we offer thee our homage of service and praise, we consecrate ourselves to thy worship, and with transports of joy embrace a state of life where everything is done under thy protection, and everyone pledges himself to praise thee, to serve thee, to proclaim thy greatness, and to defend thine Immaculate Conception. Would that our zeal for the honor of thy worship and the interests of thy glory were able to make amends to thee for all the assaults of heresy, the outrages of unbelief, and the indifference and neglect of the generality of mankind.

109

O Mother of Our Redeemer! Dispenser of all graces! extend the empire of Religion in the souls of men, banish error, preserve and increase the Faith in this country, protect innocence and preserve it from the dangers of this world and from the allurements of sin; sensible of our necessities and favorable to our desires, obtain for us the charity which animates the just, the virtues which sanctify them, and the glory which is their crown. Amen.[1]

THREE O'CLOCK PRAYER

O Divine Jesus, we transport ourselves in spirit to Mount Calvary to ask pardon for our sins which are the cause of Thy death.

We thank Thee for having thought of us in that solemn moment, and for having made us children of Thy own Mother.

Holy Virgin, show thyself our Mother by taking us under thy special protection.

St. John, be our patron and model, and obtain for us the grace of imitating thy filial piety to Mary, our Mother. Amen.

---

[1]This prayer is in the plural because it is recited in union with all those Christians throughout the world who have bound themselves in a special way to the service of Our Lady according to the spirit of Father Chaminade; namely, the Marianists—priests and Brothers of the Society of Mary, and the Daughters of Mary—their affiliated members, and their sodalists. The Three O'clock Prayer is in the plural for the same reason.

May the Father, Son, and Holy Ghost be glorified in all places through the Immaculate Virgin Mary!

PRAYER ASKING OF JESUS HIS FILIAL LOVE TOWARD MARY

O good Jesus, by the love with which Thou lovest Thy Mother, grant me, I beseech Thee, to love her truly, as Thou truly lovest her and wishest her to be loved.

O bone Jesus, rogo te, per dilectionem qua diligis matrem tuam, ut, sicut eam vere diligis et diligi vis, ita mihi des ut vere eam diligam.
—St. Anselm

If you have enjoyed this book, consider making your next selection from among the following . . .

At your bookdealer or direct from the publisher.
Prices guaranteed through December 31, 1989.

This booklet, *My Ideal—Jesus, Son of Mary*, capsulizes the way of perfect imitation of Christ through perfect imitation of His love for His Mother Mary, and it shows us how each one of us can live that message daily in a completely practical manner. For this booklet is all about the sanctification and salvation of souls. Accordingly, it is being made available at the lowest possible price for quantity distribution by the faithful to as many people as possible. The issue is the salvation of souls and peace in the world.

Quantity Discount

1 copy 3.00

5 copies 2.00 each

10 copies 1.75 each

25 copies 1.50 each

100 copies 1.25 each

500 copies 1.00 each

1,000 copies .90 each

Add $1.50 postage and handling.

Order from—

TAN BOOKS AND PUBLISHERS, INC.
P.O. Box 424
Rockford, Illinois 61105